# Two Dragons

# TWO DRAGONS

## HOWARD MARKS

### with Alun Gibbard

y Lolfa

*With thanks to Caroline Brown,*
*Marty Langford and Tee Bone Burnett,*
*and dedicated to Myfanwy Roberts*

First impression: 2010
© Howard Marks & Y Lolfa Cyf., 2010

Cover photograph: Emyr Young
Photographs by Emyr Young except the ones in
Jamaica, Patagonia and filming *Mr Nice*
Cover design: Sion Ilar

The publishers wish to acknowledge the support of
Cyngor Llyfrau Cymru

ISBN: 9 781 84771 290 5

Printed on acid-free and partly recycled paper
and published and bound in Wales by
Y Lolfa Cyf., Talybont, Ceredigion SY24 5HE
*e-mail* ylolfa@ylolfa.com
*website* www.ylolfa.com
*tel* 01970 832 304
*fax* 832 782

# CONTENTS

1

# HEARTBEATS

THE PAIN IN my upper chest got steadily worse as the evening progressed. Maybe if I went to sleep, I would wake up feeling better. I took my temple ball of Nepalese hashish, rolled the strongest joint I could, and smoked it until nothing but ash remained. Lying down on the bed, I swallowed two 20mg Valium pills. I told my girlfriend, Caroline, I was tired out, I had smoked too much dope all evening, my chest was hurting a bit, and I'd sleep it off. Unconsciousness embraced me kindly, slowly, and comfortingly. I felt good, confident I had just experienced what my mother used to refer to as a 'funny turn'.

"Nothing to worry about, Howard bach," she used to say, "It will be gone by the morning. You'll see." She was never wrong.

An hour or so later, I woke up. The pain was much sharper, spreading through my neck, down my arms, up through my jaw, into my teeth. I had implants. How could I suffer from toothache? What was going on? I moved my arm a little and felt as if an elephant had just sat down on my chest and decided to sleep there forever. The pain peaked. I couldn't handle it. I tossed, turned, and fretted. Caroline woke up.

"Are you okay, love?"

"Of course I'm fucking not. I'm in agony. Either shoot me or call the ambulance now. I can't take any more. Please."

An ambulance came within minutes. Needles, oxygen mask, thermometer, blood-pressure straps. Then those lovely words, "I think we had better give you some morphine."

"Yes, please. I've had it before. I usually need quite a lot. I have a low pain threshold. I'm not allergic to anything."

The morphine pumped into my veins, and I glided into a calm coma of comfort. I felt good. I knew the loud sirens were singing to help me, not to bang me up in prison. I was dimly aware of nurses and doctors buzzing around my stretcher, sticking pads on my chest, jabbing syringes into my stomach. Then I was on a trolley roller coasting at speed through hospital corridors, banging through double doors, twisting around corners, being examined under strong lights, connected to tomorrow's bleeping technology.

The drifting dream-like images suddenly stopped, and I woke up, sharply, and it all made sense. Jesus! I was in intensive care. I was going to die before the movie was released. I wanted to see my kids and my sister. Where was Caroline? She was right. I should never have taken all those drugs for all those years, should never have touched tequila, wallowed in whisky, popped pills, smoked spliffs, or snorted shite cocaine. I should have slowed down, taken it easy, and stopped doing shows, slept more, read more, thought more. Caroline wafted into view.

"How long have I got? Tell me the truth. I can take it. I would rather know the truth."

"What on earth are you on about? You're all right."

"What? I know what's going on. I'm hardly in intensive care because they're short of beds, am I?"

"Howard, you're not in intensive care. You are just being monitored. You'll probably be out of here in a day or so. Pull yourself together."

I felt a millisecond twinge of disappointment, then a lengthy flash of relief that still echoes through my mind today.

The consultant and his team of pupils marched in.

"Good morning, Mr Marks. I'll just read through your notes first."

He spoke to his medical students.

"Lack of oxygen causes electrical problems in the heart's conductive system, and the heart, instead of beating as it should, fibrillates. It twitches and quivers rapidly and helplessly, still alive but unable to do its job. The fibrillating heart is a sea of worms, each one with its own distinct rhythm. Unless the heart can somehow or other be reversed to enable it to pump properly, further heart attacks and death inevitably follow."

I looked up at him, knowing my eyes were sadder than ever.

"I am, of course, referring to only ventricular fibrillation. Mr Marks is suffering from atrial fibrillation, which rarely results in a fatality as long as it's attended to without delay."

Atrial fibrillation is a form of arrhythmia, when the heart's natural beat goes awry, either too fast (tachycardia) or too slow (bradycardia). Possible causes include anxiety, stress, booze, fags, caffeine, chocolate, cocaine, and chest infections. The heart's electrical system becomes confused, the heart panics and cannot beat at all.

"Mr Marks's atria are beating at 400 bpm and his ventricles are at 150 bpm. His brain and body think he's running an endless marathon."

"What can be done about it?" I asked.

"There is a variety of treatments: ablation, where we operate and disable the malfunctioning pieces of your heart; we can anaesthetise you, give you an electrical shock, and jolt it back to normality; or we could put you on beta blockers, which is what we are doing. It's the least invasive treatment."

I passed out again, thinking I had at least some chance of seeing the *Mr Nice* movie. I'll survive that long.

The sexual heart is as energetic as a man in his prime, full, erect, spurting with orgasmic power. The heart suffocates through lack of oxygen, becomes old, flabby, incapable, and turns to stone, but it never breaks. The metaphorical, metaphysical heart, however, is full of spiritual qualities; the broken heart is one of the most striking images in the human history of romantic and mystical love, whether occasioned by Cupid's careless arrows or the centurion's deity-destroying lance.

Come on, heart! You're shaped like a Welsh harp. So pluck those heartstrings, my little angels. Come on, heart! Make your noise, *dubdub, love dub, dubdub, love dub*. You're the drum that banged out God's first rhythm, alive only when beating. Cold heart, faint heart, free heart, half heart, heartburn, heart-throb, purple heart, jack of hearts, queen of hearts, sweetheart.

"What do you want, my love? We've got toast, cereal, yoghurt..."

Could I handle a hearty breakfast? Shall I eat my heart out? Images of heart-shaped food flooded my mind: tomato, avocado, guava, bunches of grapes, squid, and those crustacean love hearts from Penclawdd that are sold in Swansea market. To warm the cockles of my heart.

## 2

# SMOKE, MIRRORS, AND *MR NICE*

THE FILM *MR Nice* is now being shown in most countries, with a few notable exceptions such as the United States. In putting the film together, I'm glad the makers took heed of Alfred Hitchcock's pearl of wisdom – the length of a film should be directly related to the endurance of the human bladder.

The filming took place in 105 different locations, and I was allowed to be on set as often as I wished. Bernard Rose, the director, whose credits include *Candyman* and *Anna Karenina*, always welcomed me, as did Rhys Ifans, who is far too professional to worry about the real Howard Marks being on set.

The locations for the film were split between south Wales and Spain. Every other country in the world that played a part in the screenplay had to be recreated in one of these two countries. America was not an option as I'm not allowed to go there, and they probably wouldn't take too kindly to a film being made of my exploits which used their God-given country. There is still no distribution deal for *Mr Nice* in the USA. Although I've been released from prison, I'm still technically on parole. So if I set foot on American soil, even to change planes, and they know I've committed an offence since being released – such as smoking a joint – I can be arrested again and put back behind bars to serve out the rest of my twenty-five year sentence. I'm still a criminal in their eyes, which occasions difficulties in promoting a film about my life in their country.

In addition to the filming in Wales and Spain, Bernard Rose had tenaciously acquired original media footage of news coverage relating to different parts of my story to work in with the original material being shot, utilising green screens to mix the footage. Wales would be Wales itself, as well as the location for anything that happened in Ireland and Oxford. All border scenes, road and air, were shot at the RAF base in St Athan's near Barry in the Vale of Glamorgan. Spain was California and Pakistan. Terre Haute Prison was an old warehouse just outside Alicante.

When it came to filming in Wales, Bernard had the idea of using the house where I was born, where many scripted events actually took place, in Heol Waunbant, Kenfig Hill. Due to a combination of production practicalities and family sensitivities, it never happened. Understandably, some of my family members thought that using our home might be a step in the wrong direction – opening up our private world just that little bit too much. The film company thought the house might be unsuitable for the filming because it offered the wrong kind of look, not similar enough to a typical mining village home or what they felt one should look like.

I was asked at one point in pre-production to play the part of my father. It seemed a good idea to me because I knew him better than anyone else alive, and I could see the sense of it. And I would get paid. The idea, however, met with a frosty reception from other family members, who felt it inappropriate. The idea was shelved and rightly so.

Kenfig Hill was punctuated with chapels, schools and coal mines. There are precious few of the latter left these days, but one was needed for the authentic recreation of the village of my childhood days, so the cameras headed for the valleys to a museum housed in a former mine. The Rhondda Heritage Museum has been built around the old Lewis Merthyr colliery in Trehafod at the mouth of the Rhondda valley. It is now one of Wales's most popular tourist attractions. Coal tourism has become our legacy for feeding the furnaces of the world for decades.

The terraced Trehafod streets, hastily thrown

together when coal was first discovered there the century before last, still lie in the shadow of the winding wheel, stretching out from the valley floor up the slopes of the surrounding hills. It would do perfectly as the Kenfig Hill in which I grew up.

The first filming I attended was at Atlantic College in St Donat's Castle on the south Wales coast. It's the former home of American newspaper magnate Randolph Hearst, who first came across both the castle and Wales in an article in *Country Life* magazine. He bought St Donat's as a love gift for the American actress with whom he was having an affair, Marion Davies. In the castle, he entertained Charlie Chaplin, Douglas Fairbanks and a youthful John F Kennedy as well as Winston Churchill and George Bernard Shaw, who was extremely impressed with the place, and made some typical comment about it being the type of place that God would buy if he had enough money.

For Bernard Rose's purposes, it doubled up as Balliol College, Oxford, having the appropriate splendour and dignity. I didn't see much the day I visited as they were filming orgy scenes, which are shot traditionally without a crew of spectators within touching distance of all the frivolity. I did, however, see Rhys for a brief while and asked him how things were going.

"Today, Howard, I'm going to make you a legend in the sack!"

I'm sure he needed some chemical assistance, but I still don't know how many tablets of Viagra he had to take. He won't tell me.

A biopic, such as *Mr Nice*, is the true story of a specific person. But the balance of reality and make believe tipped one way, then the other, then back again, throughout filming. The first example of such a blurring was in the Rhondda, in Trehafod, the village that portrayed old Kenfig Hill.

Bernard Rose asked if I wanted to see the filming of me being kidnapped, which took place in a terraced house that, coincidentally, was similar to my grandmother's house. I met the two actors who were to play my parents. My father was played by William Thomas, an experienced and respected Welsh actor. My mother was played by Sarah Sugerman, the north Wales actress, who starred in *Very Annie Mary*. I found her attractive, which meant I was close to fancying my own mother.

There were further complications. Sarah Sugerman is also the first wife of David Thewlis, who plays IRA man McCann and is now living with Anna Friel. Ironically, David Thewlis is often mistaken for Rhys Ifans. People regularly approach David saying they thought he was great in *Notting Hill*. So, there I was, watching myself being kidnapped, vaguely fancying my mother who also was McCann's first wife. It was too much to take even if stoned.

Wattstown Social Club in the Rhondda was the scene of a brilliant day's filming. It was recreated as the club where I ventured on stage with my impersonation of Elvis and where I was arrested by the village police for under-age drinking. Rhys was filmed acting my impersonation of Elvis. In order to do that, first we had to record Rhys's voice for him to mime to on set. We did so in the Super Furries' studio in Cardiff, where matters tend to proceed at a leisurely pace. There's a lot of waiting for this and that to either arrive or be done. Bernard Rose, brilliant a director as he is, was not at ease with such procrastination, and his agitation became increasingly apparent as time went on. Finally, he snapped.

"Oh come on! Let's get a move on. I have another film to do after this, you know."

"You're in our world now, Bernard," was Rhys's instant laid-back reply, "You're in our world. This could take two years."

Back in Wattstown, we had a riot of a day with the locals, but the scene itself, like so many others, ended up on the cutting room floor. The same social club was used for the Irish pub scenes as well. Several local people were extras in the Rhondda valley scenes. The event generated much interest throughout the community, which consistently manifested warmth and welcome in the same way it did when people from diverse backgrounds, countries, and cultures responded to the strong pull of economic necessity and teemed into this small, narrow strip of Wales to pay homage to Old King Coal.

Recreating that world, which was nearer to the Wales of my upbringing than how it is now, required significant cooperation from those who make the Rhondda what it is today. Satellite dishes had to be pulled down – or avoided on camera shots if they weren't moveable – as did every sign of twenty-first century life, while Zephyr Zodiacs and knitted tea cosies had to be brought in.

Rhys had rented an apartment in Cardiff Bay while filming *Mr Nice*. These buildings are fairly sterile when first acquired, so Rhys's instruction to one of the production crew was quite clear.

"Stone it up a bit, Rowey, will you?"

In came Jimmy Hendrix posters, incense, ashtrays, a few rugs and whatever else Rowey thought appropriate. The stoning complete, we would regularly retire to the apartment after a day's filming, usually via James Street's White Hart pub in Tiger Bay. This infamous area achieved notoriety in 1988 when Cardiff prostitute Lynette White was found stabbed over fifty times in a room above a bookie on James Street. Three men were acquitted of the murder after spending three years in jail. Following the release of the Cardiff Three, fifteen people were charged with perverting the course of justice, thirteen of whom were police officers – the largest number of officers ever charged for such an offence following a quashed conviction.

"Whatever you do, boy, don't go in to the White Hart, ever." That's what Rhys was told when he first had his apartment down the bay. So, of course, that's exactly where he went. We became regulars and befriended Wibs from Radio Cardiff, who interviewed Rhys, the Super Furries and me at the same time on his popular show. We told all of Cardiff how much of a good time we were having, and within minutes, over a hundred listeners came to the studio and squeezed in through the door to join in. Long after the filming was over, I did a free show in the White Hart to say thank you for the way they looked after us during the shoot.

One of the most surreal smudges of film and reality happened when I wasn't on set. Cardiff Crown Court, for the purposes of the film, doubled up as the Old Bailey – the scene of one of my most notorious trials. We had used Welsh extras almost exclusively throughout the filming in the area, and a jury had to be picked from them. Some members of my family (my daughter Francesca and cousin Lynwen) were among the twelve. Another daughter, Amber, who is a criminal defence barrister, played the clerk of the court.

Also on the jury's bench was a former employee from Kenfig Hill known as Psychic Dave. In the original case I was charged with smuggling 15 tonnes of Colombian cannabis. I protested that I was actually working for the Mexican Secret Service and was acquitted, astonishingly. Psychic Dave was one of my co-defendants and is still on the run for the very same charge. He sat proudly and fearlessly on the jury that re-enacted the case. He should have been in the dock. I knew he, at least, would acquit me.

The jury were called in to deliver the verdict. Bernard and the actors built up the precisely correct degree of tension. The clerk of the court, my daughter, asked if they had reached a verdict. On being answered in the affirmative, she then asked what that verdict was.

"Guilty," said the foreman.

"Cut," said Bernard, "you're supposed to say 'Not guilty', for Christ's sake."

"Of course he's guilty. It's bloody obvious he is. I don't believe that pack of lies about working for the Mexicans. It's bullshit!"

The foreman was adamant and carried on ranting for several minutes. The set was cleared and a new foreman chosen, who this time delivered the scripted verdict of 'Not guilty'.

Apart from my vaguely fancying my mother, the other surprises were to do with my wives. One was left out completely and the other two were mixed into each other. It confused me and one of my daughters, Myfanwy, who felt awkward and upset. Her mother, Rosie, is not in the film and it's suggested throughout that Judy is Myfanwy's mother. It sounds simple enough, and for the film it might well be, but in real life it wasn't. Judy is the mother of Amber, Francesca and Patrick. On hearing that this was happening, Myfanwy came to me and asked, "So mum is airbrushed out, then?" To which there was only one reply, albeit a hurtful one. Rosie and I never fell out even though we separated when I had to go on the run. She was not someone who should have been omitted.

Ilze, my first wife, and Judy, the mother of my other three children, were both in the film as separate characters, but stories related to either one were sometimes given to the other.

"I taught you to play Go," Ilze exclaimed on seeing the director's viewing of the film. "It was me, not Judy."

It was not a massive upset, but an expression of concern and something unexpected to deal with.

The film itself is technically fascinating. Bernard Rose didn't want to put any captions on screen saying things like 'Karachi 1980'. He wanted people to know there was a change of era and location according to the style used in the film, even down to the millimetre of film used. And that had to be of its period. The film turns from black and white to colour at the point I smoke my first joint – my own Dorothy moment.

During the filming in Alicante, I was offered an opportunity to play another part in the film, this time as a coffee shop manager in Amsterdam. I would serve Rhys – in other words, me – with hash. Patrick, my son, was given a part as someone sitting in the café pretending to smoke a joint. Patrick flew there from Palma and I went there from home for the filming. It was an odd experience: there we were, Rhys and I face to face, he being me and my son sitting down nearby being someone else. But the scene was shot only to join others on the cutting room floor. Bernard was once again very apologetic and came to see me to explain why. I was afraid I'd messed it up, but Bernard's reasoning was sensible.

"Rhys has spent so much time and worked so hard to look like you and to develop your mannerisms it seems wrong that he then comes face to face with you. It doesn't look right and it draws the wrong sort of attention."

Even though Rhys was playing me forty years younger than I was during the filming, I could see what he meant. Patrick was furious about it and any explanation was completely lost on him. His mother, Judy, did however appear in the film as an American immigration officer.

The best story about the filming in Spain ended up being told to Jonathan Ross. Rhys was on the show to plug *The Boat that Rocked* but he quickly started talking about *Mr Nice*. He told Jonathan that he had been preparing to film a Harry Potter movie while filming *Mr Nice*.

"The people from the Harry Potter film flew out to Spain to measure me for my wizard costume," Rhys told Jonathan Ross, "So I'm in this room with the big pointy sleeves, the hat, the lot and Howard wanders past the room puffing at the little feller he had on the go and he said, 'I never used to wear stuff like that.' 'No, no, don't panic, How. These are the people from the Harry Potter film.' 'Oh! Pleased to meet you. Howard Marks, Hairy Pothead.'"

Rhys's involvement in the film and in my life is absolutely crucial. He plays an integral part in re-uniting me with the land of my birth, the land of my fathers and my mother. It had to be he who played me, thirteen years after our first meeting and the gentleman's agreement made by us. Rhys took me through the door back to my Welsh roots.

It was a completely different type of person – Tee Bone – who opened that door for me in the first place.

3

# A CELL, YOGA, AND TEE BONE

THE FILM, *Mr Nice*, is based on my book of the same name (the ninth non-fiction bestseller of 1997), which documents accurately my time in Terre Haute Prison and my reasons for being there. It describes in detail the racketeering, the smuggling, the dealing, the drugs, the police investigations, and the court cases. I've now seen the film several times, and it captures the emotions I went through better than the book. Sitting in auditoriums watching it, I do not relive the story: I find myself sharing the feelings with the audience.

There are references to my roots in the film, such as self-styled IRA activist Jim McCann's query as to why a Welshman should be dealing in drugs rather than painting road signs. Jim was always mindful of my Welshness, knowing it made me different from the Establishment he fought against.

There's never been a shortage of hype, attention, debate, falling out, bigotry, ignorance, and opinions about my incarceration. But being locked up in a foreign jail would require me to face a variety of other matters. Other people, other situations and alien circumstances would begin to define me. I hadn't foreseen any of them.

According to my incarcerators, I was immensely powerful in several countries and headed a 300-strong 'cartel' of dope peddlers, traffickers, mules, forgers, hookers, racketeers, terrorists, money launderers, bent cops, and other corrupt government employees. In fact, I was a 45-year-old, round-shouldered, pot-bellied, physically weak, absolutely skint, Welsh working-class smart arse with a few useless and unused qualifications from Oxford and four currently fatherless children. I was 5,000 miles from home without a single friend, family member, or fellow European anywhere near. The absence of my close family, who were too old, too young or not allowed to visit me, was tearing my heart out. I was confined within a small area surrounded by razor wire fences, searchlights, electric fences, and patrolling uniformed psychopaths itching to use their machine guns. My fellow inmates were mafia hit men, urban guerrillas, child molesters, serial killers, cannibals, rapists, mass murderers, snitches, and other perverts whose pleasure derived from other's pain. I had no choice when it came to food, clothing, employment, bed time, waking up time, work time, interior decoration, or room-mate. I had no television, radio, sound system, computer, telephone, and no female body in sight. I had no alcohol, no drugs. I was in the United States Penitentiary, Terre Haute, Indiana, the only federal penitentiary with its own Death Row.

Federal prisons take care of those offenders deemed to be either particularly threatening to national security, psychopathically uncontrollable, or otherwise inconvenient, that is, Indian braves, Islamic terrorists, bank robbers, presidential assassins, spies, interstate hooker transporters, drug smugglers, and any state convict too butch for the state authorities to handle. Federal prisons are of several different security levels based on features such as the presence of external patrols, gun towers, walls, fences, and detection devices. The federal prison with the worst reputation for slaughter and gang rape was Terre Haute. Known as 'Terror Hut', it was America's gladiator school and provided an arena for black inner city gang leaders, bikers, and nutcases.

One of the most formidably powerful black Muslim street gangs ever is the El Rukhn gang of Chicago, formerly the Blackstone Rangers.

The gang had been shrewdly financed by Libya's Colonel Kaddafi, boasted membership of thousands, and owned large real estate holdings arising through a wide range of criminal operations. Other Chicago gangs had sprung off from the Blackstone Rangers, including the Vicelords, who presently had the stranglehold on prison life in Terror Hut.

Sometimes the Vicelords got on with the El Rukhns at Terror Hut. Sometimes they didn't. Many members of Los Angeles's two notorious rival street gangs, the Bloods and the Crips, were too much for the Californian authorities to handle. They were sent to Terror Hut. Perennially fighting Washington DC Blacks had proved to be uncontrollable in the city's infamous Lorton prison. They were sent to Terror Hut. Neither the Vicelords nor the El Rukhns got on with Crips or the Bloods or any of the DC gangs. Each gang had its own peculiarities of vocabulary, its own colours, and its own system of elaborate hand signals. Different from the American city street gangs and hating them with a passion were the Jamaican Posse gangs.

There were white prison gangs too: the fanatically racist Aryan Brotherhood, the equally racist Dirty White Boys, the red-necked Dixie Mafia, the Mexican Mafia, innumerable Cuban, Puerto Rican, and Colombian syndicates, various biker gangs, and the most well-known members of the Irish and Italian Mafiosi.

One was expected to show allegiance to one particular gang. Rules of prison gang initiation varied. Some would require the execution of a random killing within the prison. The only way to avoid gang membership (or random selection for death) was to try to look and behave like an outer space alien and get noticed. I remembered how glad I'd been to be somewhat notorious when, ten years earlier, I had been first banged up at Her Majesty's Prison, Brixton. Countless TV reports, coupled with radio news reports, had assured I would be accorded a notorious criminal's welcome from notable legends of London's gangland. Could I begin to build the same friendships with the current residents of Terror Hut?

I hoped I could avoid most conflict by being nice, charming, helpful, and extremely non-macho. I was scared, for sure, but I have never known a circumstance in which it pays to manifest fear. Like jealousy, it is an emotion that must be controlled. I had been a very wimpish, squeamish kid, earnestly avoiding violence and blood. During my years at Terror Hut, I eye-witnessed gang rape, garrotting with guitar strings, heart, lung, and kidney stabbings, attempted decapitation, and a 200-strong free-for-all in which the participants were slicing each other up with homemade swords, kitchen knives, and sheets of glass. I have become numb and impassive to all forms of gore, hysteria, and grief. It's not particularly endearing to have such attributes once free, but it helped one survive in the belly of the American beast.

The inmates were supervised and refereed by tough, illiterate, obese, and red-neck United States government hacks. These guards varied from fat military megalomaniacs to fat and demented local Ku Klux Klan rejects. Their hobbies included shooting animals and brawling in bars. One had been arrested for running around naked, another for bringing in drugs, and another for participating in a pornography racket. The chaplain was busted for bringing in heroin. The warden, the man in charge, was perpetually drunk. At any other United States prison, one could be threatened with being sent to Terror Hut. Apart from the 'hole', a tiny, chilly, totally bare and spartan isolation cell which had long lost its bite due to frequency of imposition, there was no deterrent available to the Terror Hut authorities. This shortcoming often resulted in periods of mindless mayhem. At least one prisoner was stabbed every day. There would be several vicious and messy fights every day. There were plenty of murders and immeasurably more maimings. Half of those imprisoned at Terror Hut would never be released. I would probably be one of them. I could easily forget all I had learned about how to cope with a weekend in a police station, or a few weeks on remand while my friends got the bail together, or a couple of years' lay down. I had to learn how to survive being buried alive.

Classified as of the greatest severity, my offence was of maximum disrespect and insult to the American nation and community. Every day for months after the court found me guilty, I had undergone diesel therapy (shunted aimlessly around from one institution to another). I was woken at 3.00 a.m. and kept in a cold, damp, and filthy cell for three hours where I was photographed, fingerprinted, and searched at least seven times by heavily armed US marshals, who took out my dentures and dragged back my foreskin to search for my latest escape weapon. I was medically examined and injected with antibiotics. Then I was chained, manacled, handcuffed, shackled, and shuffled on board a prison bus in below zero temperatures. A padlocked black metal box chained to my waist rendered my hands further immobile. I was taken to seven different prisons during that first year. I didn't know if I was coming or going as was the intention.

At the courthouse, I was produced in the courtroom for a maximum of four hours, held in the courthouse's bullpen holding cell for several hours, and taken back to another cell, cage, or bare floor at another prison, county jail, air-force base, or army camp lock-up. I was never told where I was. I never got to sleep before midnight and I wasn't allowed any books or papers during the hours I was awake. In those conditions, I fought the US government for my freedom and lost. I had offended the sensibilities of God's very own country beyond forgiveness and had been sentenced to twenty-five years imprisonment. The only guaranteed way I could have avoided decades of prison was to have testified against my family and friends. My loyalties and ethics would have had to be replaced by obedience to the laws and regulations of God's own country.

I would have had to become a grass, a snitch, a snake, a roll-over, a stool-pigeon, a squealer, a rat, a traitor, a wrong 'un, a betrayer, a Judas, and lie at the bottom of Dante's hell for all eternity. And never ever again be able to look my parents or kids in the eyes. I couldn't do that. I would have preferred to give up the ghost and lay down in the prison cemetery, the graveyard of those forgotten before they die. If, as seemed certain, I failed to get parole, I would have to serve at least sixteen years. No one could wait for me that long.

At the age of sixty, I would re-enter the world without the proverbial pot to piss in, full of hate, and completely unemployable and useless. No one would want to listen to my boring tales of woe, gore, violence, and depression. I'd be old and ugly. No one would want to shag me. When I get out my kids will all have left home and been replaced by my grandchildren. We'll visit my parents' graves. I'll smile benignly at the children of ex-wives and their current husbands when I pay them a social call after collecting my dole or my pension. I'll walk past throbbing clubs and try to remember when I last danced.

Was it worth waiting for? Why not end it all now? Hang it up. What's so good about surviving in shit and anticipating misery? Was there anything positive and meaningful left in my life? I should at least have a search. What was I? Where had I come from? What did I have left? My thoughts and my body.

I had to do something with both or with either one. I had to at least try to deal with the fights, the conflicts going on inside me, the thoughts and feelings swirling incessantly in my mind. So I started to look after my body. There is no lack of motivation to keep fit among prisoners. Those who are sentenced to life imprisonment wish to live longer in the hope the law might eventually change and allow them amnesty. Old lags doing seriously lengthy stretches see exercise as a way to recapture those years of robbed freedom, and attempt to increase their longevity to such an extent that, by the date of release, their life expectancy is the same as it was on the day of arrest. I should at least try that, if only to keep alive the perennial daydreaming of escape: scaling fences, jumping across gun towers, and disarming prison officers, all of which requires dedicated preparation and a high level of fitness.

Most of the time my unexpected yearning for a healthier life needed to be satisfied within the confines of a tiny cell. The circumstances were ideal for the practice of yoga, the oldest system in the world of combined mind and body development.

Luckily, books on yoga are commonplace, even in prison. At first glance, the basic postures, asanas, seemed little more than a series of strange physical positions that might keep the body lean and flexible. I found them surprisingly easy to learn. At the same time, I found the yogic breathing exercises, pranayama, to be extremely calming and relaxing, and they helped me meditate, to ignore, rather than collect, my thoughts. Series of asanas might be high on providing bodily flexibility, but are considered to be fairly low on providing strength and don't even feature in the stamina ratings. Some of this can be rectified by the yoga practice of Surya Namaskara, the sun salutation, which is a graceful sequence of twelve positions dynamically executed as one continuous exercise. I had to ignore the books' suggestion to perform this sequence at the side of a large lake or river while staring into the dawn. In prison, one learns to compromise.

I'd like to keep spiritual matters and religion well out of this, so I'm not going to rave about inner peace, essential nature, or harmony. Quite simply, yoga made sense: stretching and breathing, as opposed to contracting and puffing, and overcoming the physical discomfort generated by some of them gave a sweet, calming feeling. Although I have never thought it's the least bit important to avoid chemical highs, it was comforting to realise that there are other ways of achieving similar mental states.

Despite the vaguely energetic dynamics of some of its practice, yoga is perceived by most American prisoners to be hippie, drippy, or sissy. Consequently, other forms of exercise are constantly searched for by those living in cells. One that was new to me, and from which I greatly and clearly benefited, was callisthenics, which necessitate no special equipment and use only one's own weight as resistance. Mere body weight is enough to start a basic callisthenics routine, but the exercises may be modified to accommodate difficulties in starting, when the body weight may be too much. They may also be modified to increase resistance once the exercises become too easy. An obvious example is a press-up. It can be made easier by starting off on your knees. Gravitational resistance can be increased by elevating one's feet on a chair to increase the proportion of weight on the upper body. In stomach work (sit-ups, crunches and leg raises), upper body work (chin-ups), and leg work (calf raises and side leg raises), varying resistance is obtained in the number of repetitions done. Most of the exercises work a variety of muscle groups, thus few exercises are needed to maintain a base level of fitness. Callisthenics lose their value when performed too fast. One has to keep the exercises slow enough to feel the muscles work. Furnishing a focus on control and technique is added to the expected increase in strength and muscle tone.

Neither basic callisthenics routines nor yogic asanas increase cardiovascular capacity, so I accompanied them with an aerobic programme such as running on the spot or swinging my arms. A brisk walk through the countryside or manic dancing under strobe lights would have been better.

As the months ticked by, the prison authorities began to perceive me as someone who could be trusted to leave my cell for increasingly longer periods and be treated as a regular prisoner. Long-term prison routine is generally structured to allow a typical inmate to use an extensive selection of exercise facilities (which would shame most British health clubs) for about fifty hours a week. There was an indoor and outdoor gymnasium, weightlifting shacks, tennis courts, squash courts, football fields, basketball courts, and jogging tracks. Those who wished to exercise even more could usually secure an appropriate prison job assisting the daily maintenance of the services. I simply played as much tennis as possible and walked around the jogging track when the courts were full, but some prisoners in these circumstances can, and do, achieve remarkable standards of physical fitness. Recently, United States' governments have enacted statutory and regulatory measures to deprive inmates of this health bonanza. Certain taxpayers are not enthusiastic about funding the long-term transformation of an unhealthy, confused, and possibly feeble delinquent into a fit, powerfully-built man, tightly focused on revenge against the system that destroyed everything he had.

Exercising worked, and happiness seemed to serendipitously ooze into my mind. I was surviving better, even if I still didn't really know who I was.

Then I started realising I was Welsh.

Since the day of my arrest, none of the guards

or inmates had paid a blind bit of notice to my Welshness. It was hardly surprising. I was always reading English publications and, unlike them, spoke the language like a native. Occasionally, I would mention I was Welsh but was inevitably faced with either disbelieving or glazed and disinterested eyes whenever I tried to explain what it meant. My listeners could never accept that Welsh was its own unique language, that it wasn't an English dialect, that Princess Diana wasn't Welsh, or that the Welsh were Britain's original inhabitants.

Then one day, Tee Bone, a fellow prisoner convicted of killing policemen and distributing crack cocaine, told me he had listened to a programme about the Welsh on his radio, which stated that Hilary Clinton, soon to be America's First Lady, was of Welsh descent on both sides of her family. Tee Bone went on to say he didn't remember much of the programme but from what he could gather, the mother of Bob Hope, his favourite comic, was Welsh, as were five of the first six American presidents, including Thomas Jefferson, and eighteen signatories of the Declaration of Independence. Outlaw Jesse James, bank robber Pretty Boy Floyd, and Murray 'the Camel' Humphries, the first gangster to 'stand on the Fifth' were Welsh.

I had never heard any of this and doubted

its veracity. I simply didn't believe Tee Bone. He must have got it wrong. But I had to check. I could not stand the shame of knowing less about Wales than a random Chicago crack dealer convict who had not a drop of Welsh blood in his veins. Prisoners were allowed to borrow books from local libraries. I ordered several, all of which dealt with the connections between Wales and America, and I read them all.

Tee Bone's memory had served him well. Hilary Clinton's parents, Dorothy Howell and Hugh Rodham were Welsh. America's first president, George Washington, wasn't, but his wife, Martha, was. The next five presidents (John Adams, Thomas Jefferson, James Madison, James Monroe, and John Quincy Adams) were Welsh. So were Pretty Boy Floyd, Jesse James, and Murray 'the Camel' Humphries.

Suddenly, America stopped being such an alien country. It was full of us Welsh, to whom it seemed to owe its very existence.

The night I left Oakdale Detention Centre and started the physical journey back to Wales, eight others left the same time as me: an Americanised Nigerian of British nationality and seven South Americans.

"Is this all your property, Marks?"

I had approximately one hundred dollars, a pair of shorts, nail clippers, comb, toothbrush, alarm clock, papers confirming my 'release' date of two weeks ago, a credit card I could use in prison vending machines, and five books, including one written about me, *Hunting Marco Polo*.

"Yes, that's it."

I put the money in my pocket. It felt strange. First time in over six years. How often was I going to be thinking that? First time in over six years. Money, sex, wine, a joint of marijuana, a bath, an Indian curry. All around the corner.

My other belongings were put into a cardboard box. I was given a pair of blue jeans with legs about a foot too long and an extremely tight, white T-shirt. This was called being 'dressed out', a gift from the United States government for those re-entering the free world.

We were handcuffed, but not chained, and squeezed into a small van. Then we picked up two other guys from another prison exit. One seemed Hispanic, the other seemed northern European. Everyone was silent, excited by his own thoughts. The van's engine made a terrible racket as it headed towards Houston with the dawn, just beginning to break. By 9 o'clock, it was like sitting on a rock in a sardine can on fire. By 10 o'clock, we were sitting in an enormous holding cell at Houston International Airport, along with over fifty other criminal aliens.

The northern European asked the Nigerian, "Where do you live?"

His accent was strong south Walian. I had never met a Welshman in an American prison, nor heard of one. I'd met very few Americans who'd heard of Wales.

"Are you Welsh?" I interrupted.

"Aye," he said, looking at me with deep suspicion.

"So am I."

"Oh yeah?" Deeper suspicion.

"Which part are 'ew from?" I asked, laying on the accent a bit.

"Swansea," he said, "and 'ew?"

"Twenty-five miles away from 'ew in Kenfig Hill," I answered.

He started laughing.

"You're not him are you? God Almighty! Jesus Wept! Howard bloody Marks. Marco fucking Polo. They're letting you go, are they. That's bloody great. Good to meet you, boy. I'm Scoogsie."

We had a chat, a long one. Scoogsie explained how he, too, had just finished a drug sentence, and he told me of his early days in the business.

"My wife has worked for a long time in a drug rehabilitation centre in Swansea. Not a bad partnership, really. I get them hooked; she gets them off. We keep each other going, like."

Memories of south Walian humour had often helped me through the bad times in prison. Now I was hearing it for real. I was heading back towards my roots, and they were reaching out for me.

Looking confused, the Nigerian belatedly replied to Scoogsie's original question.

"I live in London. I am being deported there. I am never coming back here. They took away my money, my property, and my business. Just because someone I didn't know swore in court that I sold him some drugs."

An all too familiar story. The number of deportees in the converted aeroplane hangar was dwindling.

"Anyone else going to London?" Scoogsie asked.

No one.

Soon, there were just the three of us left. We'd found out that the Continental Airlines flight to London should be leaving in an hour. An immigration officer came in holding a gun.

"This way, you three."

A small van took us to the gangway. With his gun, the immigration officer indicated we should climb the steps. The Nigerian led the way. Scoogsie followed and spat dramatically on American soil.

"None of that!" ordered the immigration man, waving his gun.

"Don't mess it up now, Scoogsie. You know what they're like."

"I know what the fuckers are like, all right," said Scoogsie. "I hate them. I wouldn't piss in their mouths if their throats were on fire. I'm never going to eat another McDonalds. No more cornflakes for breakfast. And pity help any Yank who asks me the way anywhere. Let anyone dare try to pay me in dollars. God help him."

"Take it easy, Scoogsie. Let's get on board."

I never saw him again.

# 4

# THE COALMINE, THE IRISH, AND THE OPEN SEAS

MY FIRST LINK back to my Welsh roots was seeing my family again. It was a wonderful experience. They, too, felt it tough when I was not only in prison but also thousands of miles away in America. I lost my dear father, Dennis Marks, less than two years after being released from prison. He had been ill for a long time, but nothing could kill him until his son was free.

He was the son of a collier who earned some extra shillings fighting his way through the boxing booths of south Wales. If any one could last a whole round with Tudor Marks without getting knocked out, Tudor would give them a few shillings. If not, he kept the money. Tudor's grandfather, Patrick McCarty, had moved from Cork to Kenfig Hill, near Bridgend in south Wales. He had a dark past, to say the least, and his life was full of questions before he came to Wales but there were very few answers.

There was one rather obvious question. How did a Marks have a paternal grandfather called McCarty? Why did he change the family name to Marks? Every single member of the family who came over with him had to do the same, they didn't have a choice. Of course, in the land of the twitching curtains, the neighbours were quite ready to offer their own interpretations. Maybe he was on the run from the police in Ireland because he'd committed a terrible crime. Maybe he wanted to inherit money from the German Jews who owned the local colliery. Maybe, others suggested, some family member had brought shame on the family name and it just had to be changed. But the bottom line was nobody really knew.

Tudor had married Katie Jones, the local midwife. She'd brought over two thousand babies into this world. Her father, also a collier, was once trapped underground following a horrific accident. He managed to stay alive by drinking horse piss. That turned out to be one of those family stories that cropped up every year, usually at Christmas, told as if it had never been told before. Usually, we managed to fake our response as kids until one year we'd had enough and ended the story for my mother, who immediately expressed her surprise as to how we knew what had happened.

In his teens, my father had left the area in order to start a career with the navy. He first went to the Cardiff Nautical College. The good, prosperous days in Cardiff docks had started in the 1880s when the world was desperate for Welsh anthracite coal. It was the best coal for ships and the new industries. Cardiff was the base for over a hundred and twenty shipping companies and housed the world's only coal exchange, where the price of coal was set by a cartel of coal industrialists and where the world's first million pound cheque was signed.

Cardiff's largest shipping line was Reardon Smith Line which was established by Irishman Sir William Reardon (O'Riordean) Smith. In 1929 my father joined his company as an apprentice. Within ten years he was the merchant navy's youngest captain. During the Second World War he was Fleet Commodore, responsible for leading weapon-carrying convoys from Milford Haven to the British forces all round the world. I still have his medals.

When the war was over, my father was made captain of the 10,000-tonne cargo ship, the *SS Bradburn*. He travelled around the world again, this time carrying a whole variety of goods.

He was away at sea when I was born in 1945, coming to the end of his twenty-one years with the Merchant Navy. I was 2 years old when I met him for the first time. Now and again, the company was willing for my father to take my mother with him on some of his voyages. In 1948, the company was willing for me to go with them as well and, as a result, by the time I was 5, I had visited almost every country in the world.

Back home, most people in the locality spoke English from day to day. But my mother was an exception. Her mother came from the Swansea valley and as a result her first language was Welsh and it was my first language as well. I didn't speak English until I was 5 years old, having to pick it up on going to a primary school where only about 5 per cent of the children spoke Welsh. Turning to speak English, therefore, proved to be an easy and natural thing to do and it wasn't long before I was more comfortable and eloquent in the English language than in Welsh.

I spoke only Welsh with my mother. She would correct me if I used any of my freshly acquired English vocabulary. One day, my father decided that he too wanted to learn Welsh, but as my Welsh remained better than his, we spoke only English to each other. A year later, my sister was born. Both my parents and I spoke only Welsh to her. And to round it off, my parents spoke only English to each other. Looking back, it was quite a complicated set up but we seemed to get by and understood each other.

I have no recollection whatsoever of being taught anything about the English oppression of Wales. My parents and other adults around me through my growing years had always given me the impression England was a strong, powerful, friendly country. As Welsh people we were dependent on England for our existence as a country. In school, we had learned of the abject failure of Owain Glyndŵr to withstand the attacks of the all-conquering Anglo-Normans and from then on, the two countries had been inseparable friends. Wales didn't have a capital city; road signs and all official documents and forms were in English. Wales was a region and the Welsh were the English of the west.

England was certainly not an enemy. That label was exclusively for two other countries in the world, Germany and Japan. Second World War hostilities might well have ended, but we still had the ration books, and we boys made sure that in our games and comics, the spirit of war would live on.

Nevertheless, we were aware of differences. We could sing better for a start. But the Welsh weren't singing songs I liked. The English had sex and glamour. We had sheep and chapels. The English played better football than we did. Wales had just four teams in the four divisions of the Football Association's League – Cardiff, Newport, Swansea, and Wrexham. We had only one highly acclaimed player, John Charles, and he lost no time in scarpering from Cardiff to

Leeds. The Welsh, however, were particularly good at rugby, and it has always been essential we beat England in that sport, at least.

That's when the emotions would turn into a hotbed of stirred up frenzy. I remember my grandfather smashing the radio to bits with his hobnailed boots because Wales had missed a crucial, easy penalty. But all this was a rivalry, an enmity on the playing fields and nowhere else. Wales won the Grand Slam in 1952 but there was not a real deal of celebration as we took our place side by side with the English to mourn the death of King George VI. His grandson would be Wales's next prince, the first since Edward VIII in 1910. It appeared we were proud of the fact. The following year, we would stand in the queue leading from the front door of the one family in our street who had a television so we could watch a new queen being crowned.

There were more coal mines than schools and more chapels than pubs in Kenfig Hill and my mother had taught me, quite definitely, to stay out of those pubs. That was no problem until I reached my teens. She also taught me, with the same degree of foreboding, to stay away from the pits. I was not warned against going to chapel, quite the opposite. I had to go even though I hated it. I went to school, however, fairly willingly.

Apart from my sister Linda, I had only one real friend, Marty Langford, whose father owned the multi-award-winning ice-cream shop in the village. Marty and I were very similar, sharp enough in the classroom but also popular enough outside. Each of us could hold our own when fighting in the schoolyard.

While I was waiting for the results of my 11+ exam, I decided to be ill. School was boring and, more importantly, I needed a little sympathy and attention. Just before falling 'ill' I had discovered it was possible to flick the mercury in the thermometer with my finger in order to make it rise. So, when no one was looking, I would decide what temperature I wanted to be and flick accordingly. If anyone had looked at the thermometer carefully they would have seen there was an obvious gap in the mercury line, showing clearly what I had done. But no one did notice. I became an expert at faking sore throats, nausea and all sorts of other symptoms, and my temperature could rise to anything up to 104 degrees Fahrenheit.

Fevers that cause dramatic rises and falls in temperature are very rare. One such illness is undulant fever, also known as Gibraltar Fever or Rock Fever. Apparently, the Apostle Paul suffered from it, as did as my father.

With the idea of such a disease firmly

implanted in my parents' minds, it soon became the only possible explanation to them of what was wrong with me. I was put in an isolation ward on my own in Bridgend General Hospital. I loved it. Dozens of doctors and nurses swarmed around my bed throughout the day, each one showing immense kindness to me as they carried out all sorts of tests.

Foolishly on their part, they left me on my own with the thermometer fairly regularly. So it was very easy to create another fever. There was also plenty of time to look through the file at the end of my bed labelled 'Not to be handled by the patient'. I quickly developed a serious interest in all things medical and an even greater interest in nurses.

After some weeks of drugs and sex in the guise of medication and nurses, I was totally bored once again. I really needed to go back home to play with my Mecano set. I gave up tampering with the thermometer and stopped complaining as well. Unfortunately, the hospital proved far more difficult to leave than to get into – a little bit like prison. I worried so much about wanting to leave, would they be willing for me to leave, and if so when would I be allowed to leave, I wasn't eating properly. As a result, I was presenting the medical profession with another symptom. Gallons of Lucozade restored my appetite. I was released from hospital and told to go home for a period of recuperation. My first scam was over.

I passed my 11+ and so did Marty. Although the nearest grammar school to Kenfig Hill was five miles away in Bridgend, for some reason the local authority sent us more than twice the distance to the Garw Grammar School, in the bleak Garw valley. Garw means rough or rugged and it's a dead end valley. It was an old-fashioned grammar school but, unusually, boys and girls were taught there together. The school stood opposite the Ffaldau coal mine in Pontycymer, the last village but one before the dead end.

Children from a catchment area of about 15 miles went to the Garw Grammar and my home was precisely 11 miles from the school gates. The bus – which we called 'yellow dog' because it stopped at every lamppost – took over an hour to get there. Nothing, therefore, happened outside school hours. There was the obligatory school uniform, but no-one wore it. The sheep from the nearby hills would come to visit us regularly, joining us on the schoolyard and occasionally in the classrooms as well. The school boasted only one well-known former pupil who had brought any degree of pride to the area, Daniel Davies, who was once the Queen's physician.

I soon gave up fighting on the schoolyard, mainly because I had lost the ability and everyone else started to win and partly because I couldn't stand any physical contact with boys. The nurses at Bridgend General Hospital had spoiled me. Bless them.

I had reason to fall back on the medical knowledge gained at that hospital once again and to rediscover my skills at flicking the mercury in thermometers. A new disease had once again come to light which meant I had to be excused from all physical exercise lessons in the school. The other boys called me all sorts of names as a result. I was a wimp, a sissy boy, a yellow belly, a chicken, and a coward. Making matters ten times worse was my doing well in the school exams – I was a swot as well.

Life wasn't going in the direction I wanted it to go. The girls ignored me, and the boys made fun of me. I needed some big changes in my life.

Obviously, Elvis Presley didn't have these problems. I'd seen his films, listened incessantly to his recordings, and avidly read everything about him. His hairstyle was my hairstyle. As much as possible, it was essential to look like him, sound like him, and move like him. I failed, but I thought I so very nearly succeeded. After all, I was thin, tall, and I had dark hair and thick lips. If I stood up straight, it was possible to lose my rounded shoulders and the gut I had.

Since I was six years old, I took twice weekly

piano lessons in the home of a neighbour. But to the great disappointment of my parents, such pieces as 'Für Elise' and 'Moonlight Sonata' were put one side, and the early morning practising to perfect such tunes was soon forgotten. I started working on performing 'Teddy Bear' and 'Blue Suede Shoes' to an imaginary audience.

In school, I decided it was time to manifest my hitherto hidden mischievous side to make me unpopular with the teachers and popular with my fellow pupils. The lack of physical toughness, however, persisted as a problem as everyone still thought I was a wimp. Subsequently, the bullying became more commonplace. I didn't have enough guts to pull out my Elvis card, so what I really needed was a bodyguard.

Most of my fellow pupils lived in the surrounding villages of the scattered coalfield community, with each community proud of its own social life and young people's scene. Very few went to the grammar school on the other side of the valley. Every village also had its hard nut, and Albert Hancock was Kenfig Hills's. He was a wild-looking teenager who bore a remarkable resemblance to James Dean.

I was used to seeing him on the streets of Kenfig Hill, but I really did fear him. Most sober people feared him. I clearly had to be friends with him somehow and I tried everything I could think of to be on his side. I bought some cigarettes for myself and asked him to show me how to inhale, I ran errands for him and I 'lent' him money. Eventually a long-term partnership developed, and suddenly all my school friends were too afraid to mock me any more. Albert's bad name and reputation had travelled far and wide. When I was 14, Albert took me to a pub for my first pint. Fortunately or otherwise there was an old piano near the bar and it caught my eye. With alcohol fuelled confidence, I walked over towards it and accompanied myself singing 'Blue Suede Shoes'. Everyone was delighted with my well-practised performance.

About a year or so later, my father found a diary I had kept containing exaggerated notes on how much I had drunk and smoked, together with a comprehensive record of my sexual exploits. His response was swift and clear: I was to be banned from going out completely. I was grounded. The only place I was allowed to go to was school. He also insisted I cut my Teddy Boy hairstyle. Thank God Elvis simultaneously had his hair cut in order to enter the US military. Part of the punishment, at least, had proven to be a blessing.

My O levels were six months away and given my grounded state, the only sensible option was to study for them, which I did with an intense degree of obsession and tenacity. I passed all ten subjects with very high grades. My parents, understandably, were delighted and the ban on going out was lifted. Albert too was, surprisingly, over the moon. He now had a best friend who was a combination of Elvis and Einstein.

My new-found freedom couldn't have been timed better. Van's Teen and Twenty Club had just opened in Kenfig Hill. Bands performed there every week and quite often, I would get an invite to sing a few songs from my very restricted repertoire – 'What'd I Say', 'Blue Suede Shoes', and 'That's All Right Mama' was just about all I could manage, but the reception was great every time. Life turned into one dependable routine. Weekdays were devoted to school work and studying but every non-working hour was devoted to drinking, dancing and singing in Van's, and taking girls out to dark alleys and haystacks.

My A level subjects were physics, chemistry and pure and applied maths. Despite being good at these subjects, I had little interest in them. I didn't have much interest in any other academic subject either. My interests were entangled with my obsessions and restricted to sex, alcohol and rock and roll. Every single one I pursued with passion and commitment.

It was, therefore, a total shock to stand in front of the headmaster and hear him say he wanted me to sit the entrance scholarship examination for Oxford. No one had attempted to go to Oxford from Garw Grammar in over eight years, and the last one to succeed was the headmaster's son, John Davies. He went to Balliol to read physics, and the headmaster suggested I do the same.

# 5

# WOOLWORTH GIRLS AND OXFORD DONS

WHEN IT WAS first suggested that I study at Oxford, I had no expectation of getting anywhere near being admitted and certainly didn't think going to such a hallowed establishment would have a deep-rooted influence on the way I saw life and the path it would follow. Oxford became my introduction to the drug world as well as my overture to attitudes towards Wales I had not heard before, safely cocooned in a valley which was as much a way of thinking as a geographical feature. I had enough of a job working out where Oxford was and why I should be going there in the first place.

Although I was aware that Oxford University comprised colleges such as Jesus and Christ Church, I had not heard of Balliol. The headmaster suggested I read Anthony Sampson's *Anatomy of Britain*. The section dealing with Balliol was impressive and intimidating. The list of Balliol men included far too many prime ministers, kings, and eminent academics to warrant my even conceiving of being admitted. However, there was nothing to lose. If I failed, I could go to University of Wales, Swansea or King's College, London, where I already had places waiting for me to take if I wished.

During the autumn of 1963, I sat the first of the Oxford University entrance examinations at my grammar school. Two sets of examination papers arrived, one on physics, which was no problem, and another general paper, which was incomprehensible. One of the questions was, 'Is a copy of *The Times* more useful than a Thucydides or a Gibbon?' I had heard of neither Thucydides nor Gibbon and had never seen a copy of *The Times*. This question remained unanswered, as did most of them. However, I did answer one on whether it was morally correct for pop singers to earn more than hospital ward sisters did. I maintained it was, mainly on the basis pop singers had no minimum wage guarantee.

Preparing for the initial interview at Balliol was a nerve-wracking experience. In those days, my hair was long, soaked in Brylcreem, and combed in a Teddy Boy style with a quiff over my forehead. My parents insisted I had a haircut, and I reluctantly complied.

I remember little about the train journey from

Bridgend to Oxford. I abandoned *Anatomy of Britain* when the train reached Cardiff and settled down in the buffet carriage to drink numerous cans of beer. I sat opposite a man holding a pair of handcuffs and, for the first time, saw the dreaming spires.

A couple of hours later I, along with another interviewee, was waiting outside Professor Bell's room in Balliol for my general interview. The other candidate asked me which school I attended. I told him.

"Where's that?" he asked.

I answered.

"Oh Wales," he said scornfully. I asked him which school he came from.

"Eton," he said, looking down at the floor. I could not resist asking, "Where's that?" but he didn't reply. I did not know Eton's geographical location, but I had heard of it.

The Etonian was the first in, and I pressed my ear against the doorframe to hear long articulate renditions of various sporting accomplishments. My apprehension increased. Despite being a rugby fan, I had not participated in any physical exercise or sports since I was twelve years old, when my school foolishly selected me to play as a second row forward for the B team. My already fragile confidence plummeted to virtual nonexistence. The Etonian exited, and the doorframe filled with the imposing figure of Professor Russell Meiggs. He was magnificent and instantly became my hero. His shoulder-length hair filled me with elation, but I now regretted acquiescing to my parents' insistence on my visiting the barber before I left Wales. Professors Bell and Meiggs made me feel completely at ease, and we talked at length about Welsh coalmines, the national rugby team, and the Eisteddfod. I made them both laugh on a number of occasions. The physics interview, however, was a much more sombre affair, and I quickly realised I could not joke my way through this one. I had read nothing outside the S level curriculum and was dreading questions about relativity or quantum mechanics, which to this day I still cannot fully understand. Luckily, all the questions lay within the A level curriculum.

A couple of months later, I was again summoned to Balliol to sit more entrance scholarship examinations. These were spread over a period of a few days, and I had to reside in the college. Despite my having explained in full detail to my parents the nature of Russell Meiggs's hairstyle, I could not avoid the mandatory haircut.

I joined the other candidates gathered in the junior common room. The Etonian was not among them. I felt shy and inhibited. Eventually,

I began talking to another grammar school boy, who was from Southampton. He, too, intended to read physics and seemed to feel as out of place as I did. His name was Julian Peto. He has remained my best friend ever since and is now professor of cancer studies at London University.

Julian and I dutifully attended the examination schools every morning and afternoon and, equally dutifully, got completely drunk every evening. Somehow, we dealt with a few more interviews, and I returned home without making any further friendships and not expecting to visit Oxford again.

During the first half of December 1963, a letter posted from Balliol arrived at my home in Wales. Full of apprehension, I gave it to my father to open. The expression of delight on his face conveyed the letter's contents. Oxford University had accepted his son.

The news I had been successful in my attempt to enter Oxford University swept through Kenfig Hill like wildfire. Balliol had just won the *University Challenge* quiz, which increased the awe and respect I was accorded. I could not walk down the street without congratulations from everyone I met. My success went completely to my head, and I have been living off it to some extent ever since.

Until beginning my first term at Balliol in

October, I spent 1964 basking in the glory of my surprising achievements. I kept my eyes open for mentions of Balliol in the media but recall only seeing one article, which described the new Balliol fad of smoking marijuana, about which I knew nothing.

Along with two very proud parents, I spent a few days in Oxford during August 1964 purchasing items needed to begin residence away from home. We visited Balliol, but it was deserted and lifeless apart from the odd American tourist staring, with unconcealed disappointment, at the gardens. All our purchases were neatly packed into the cabin trunk except for the college scarf, which I began using to improve my efficiency at hitchhiking.

During early October 1964, the big day arrived, and I began life as a fully enrolled Balliol undergraduate. My small, poky, and drab room was on the ground floor overlooking St Giles and vulnerable to inspection by passers-by. The traffic noise was the worst I had ever encountered in sleeping quarters, and the window provided me with my first, though unfortunately by no means my last, opportunity of looking at the outside world through bars. An elderly man wearing a white jacket shattered the gloom of my immediate environment. He walked in and said, "I be your scout, George." I had not heard of scouts and had no idea what function they served. My first thought was he was something to do with sports activities. George explained his duties included making my bed, cleaning my room, and washing my dishes. I had never eaten at a restaurant with waiter service, a porter had never carried my bag, and I had never stayed at a hotel. I was astonished.

Apart from Julian Peto, I found no-one among the freshmen with whom I could establish a friendship. Dining at the hall was frightening. I had no idea what to talk about and was concerned about exhibiting bad table manners. I felt out of place and miserable. Fellow diners treated me as if I was a native of some recently discovered primitive civilisation. Did we really fuck cows and sheep? Did I live somewhere where there was no electricity, telephone, television, or plumbing? To them, my Welsh accent was virtually incomprehensible. Any attempt I made at conversation was met with mocking laughter. I had to repeat every statement I made. I was ill with homesickness.

During the first few days, Julian and I attended a Freshers' Fair held at the town hall. None of the various societies and clubs, busily recruiting new members, offered anything that appealed to us. Three attractive girls approached us and invited us to join the Oxford University

Conservative Party. Julian, a member of CND and a sincere socialist born to humanist parents, walked off in disgust while I lingered, overcome by overtures of feminine charm. To prolong this enjoyable encounter, I agreed to become a Tory party member and parted with a few shillings for the privilege of doing so. My parents, on later hearing of this treachery, were livid. I did not attend any of the party's meetings and never again clasped eyes upon those three beautiful women. The only possible repercussion of this impulsive foolishness was the probability of its documentary record being favourably regarded by those ultimately responsible for recruiting me as an MI6 agent.

A day or so after the Freshers' Fair, I wandered along to the Oxford Union. Due to having attended a dance at University of Wales, Swansea's Union some months earlier, I presumed if there was any rock music, alcoholic frivolity, and promiscuity, it would be at the union, rather than anywhere else in the university. I was wrong. I paid eleven pounds for a life membership and did not visit there once. My life membership card, however, remained in my wallet until confiscated by the United States Drug Enforcement Administration in July 1988. They seem reluctant to return it to me.

The physics tutorials I was obliged to attend

were surprisingly relaxed affairs, and I managed to keep my head above water. I attended a few university lectures but soon stopped doing so when I realised that they were not compulsory. I began meeting Balliol students outside of the natural science faculty and formed the opinion that arts undergraduates, particularly historians and philosophers, were a far more interesting and non-conforming bunch than scientists were.

I joined a few Balliol societies, including the Victorian Society, where the main requirement was to down large amounts of port, which I had never tried. Each member was obliged to sing a Victorian song to the audience of other members and further obliged to sing different Victorian songs at subsequent meetings. Showing great kindness, the officers of the society permitted me to sing the same song on each occasion, a Welsh hymn, 'Wele Cawsom y Meseia', sung to the tune of 'Bread of Heaven'.

My sexual adventures confined themselves to those with females not attached to the university. I assumed that university girls were not the type to go to bed with me or anyone else. This ridiculous assumption resulted from my Welsh country upbringing, where there was no overlap of girls who studied and girls who would 'do it'. The ones that 'did it' would invariably be girls who had left school as soon as they could, and they would tend to work in Woolworth's, betting shops, or factories. Consequently, my first sexual liaisons in Oxford began in the Cornmarket Woolworth's store and the odd street encounter. Most of the latter seemed to be with girls attending nursing and secretarial colleges. This illusion of blue stocking celibacy continued until the last week of Michelmas term when, at a college society, I made a disgusting exhibition of myself by attempting to imitate Elvis Presley while the main vocalist of The Blue Monk and his Dirty Habits was taking a break. Curiously enough, because of this, I began my first affair with university undergraduate Lynn Barber of St Anne's College, to which she refers in her excellent book, *An Education*. No more Woolworth's girls. I returned to the Welsh valleys and celebrated Christmas a much happier person than the one who had left there two months earlier.

Back at Oxford, I acquired an exaggerated reputation as a womaniser. In those days there used to be a 'Bets Book' kept in the college's junior common room wherein college members would record their wagers with one another to increase the probability of the bet actually being honoured. At this time, Richard Burton and Elizabeth Taylor were participating in an OUDS production of *Doctor Faustus*. I recall being extremely flattered to read in the 'Bets Book' that someone had wagered I would succeed in seducing Elizabeth Taylor. He lost his bet. Twenty years later, I sat next to Elizabeth Taylor in the first-class cabin of a TWA flight from Delhi to Frankfurt and had an animated conversation with her for some hours. No seduction by either party was attempted.

I made friends with Henry Hodge, who later became the chief immigration judge. He spoke often of his friend Denys Irving, who had been rusticated from Oxford for a year, which he spent sensibly visiting exotic parts of the world. He had recently returned from his voyages of discovery and was about to visit his friends at Oxford. Henry invited me to meet him. Denys had brought with him some marijuana in the form of kif from Morocco. Up till then, I had heard the odd whisper of drugs being taken at the university and knew marijuana was popular with British West Indian communities, jazz enthusiasts, American beatniks, and the British intellectual wave of 'angry young men', but I hadn't tried it. Enthusiastically, I accepted the joint Denys offered and took my first few puffs.

The effects were surprisingly mild but long lasting. At first, I had a sensation of butterflies in the stomach but without the customary feelings of trepidation. This led to a desire to laugh, followed by my interpreting most of the conversation as amusing enough for me to do so. I then became acutely aware of the music (James Brown's 'Please, Please, Please') and of the aesthetic qualities of my immediate environment. My next awareness was of the slowing down of time. Finally, I became hungry, as did everyone else, and by some means of transport now long forgotten, we invaded the premises of what later became the Sorbonne French restaurant but was then the Moti Mahal. This was my first experience of Indian food, and I have been hooked on it ever since. (One never knows what cannabis can lead on to.)

After endless bhajis, kurmas, pilaos, doopiazas, and other curries, the effects of the marijuana wore off. I invited my new friends, which included Joshua Macmillan, grandson of the former prime minister and chancellor of Oxford University, and Hamilton McMillan (Mac), who later recruited me for MI6, to come back to my room in Balliol where we proceeded to re-establish our highs by numerous joints of marijuana. One by one, we passed out.

Shortly afterwards, Joshua Macmillan died from an overdose of drugs (heroin and barbiturates) and alcohol. Within a day or so of Joshua's death, my pigeon-hole contained a summons to see the dean, Francis Leader McCarthy Willis Bund, 'as soon as possible'. I went to the dean's rooms and had my first ever conversation with him. He came straight to the point. Joshua's death would trigger off inquiries by the police, journalists, and proctors (university police) into drug taking in the university, with particular emphasis on Balliol. The dean was making his own preliminary investigation and he had 'good reason' to start this investigation by asking me some questions, "Do you take drugs?" "Who else did?" "Where did they take them?" I explained I had smoked marijuana a couple of times but I was not prepared to give him names of others who may have also done so. The dean seemed so relieved at my refusal to name others, and I have not forgotten the look on his face, which has since carried me through all sorts of unpleasant interrogations.

*The Sunday Times* featured an article headlined 'Confessions of an Oxford drug addict'. Similarly themed articles appeared in other newspapers. The most unlikely students were queuing up to confess to some reporter their flirtation with Oxford's drug culture. Marijuana smokers were emerging all over the place, and it was considered fairly unfashionable not to be one. Having fortuitously penetrated the drug culture a couple of days prior to the national exposé, I acquired the status of one of its pioneers and did nothing to dispel this misconception.

The proctors summoned me to appear before them 'in connection with a confidential matter'. I immediately sought the advice of the dean, who was by now getting very concerned and anxious about all the unwelcome attention Balliol was attracting.

I developed the beginnings of an enormous liking and respect for him, and it seemed he had a fatherly affection for me. He spoke about his life, taking care to mention his former position as a proctor, and how proctors generally were a bad lot. He subtly advised me to behave with them in precisely the same way as I had done when first questioned by him. I turned up to see the proctors and refused to answer all questions on the grounds it was against my ethical code to incriminate either myself or other people. Dismissed with a "You'll hear from us later," I walked out. The dean was waiting outside. "Did you stand up to that damnable pair?" I told him I had but expressed my concern they were likely to punish me for my silence. The dean said if that should happen, then they would have to cope with his resignation. I believed him, and from then on, we had an unbreakable bond of friendship.

During the long summer holiday of 1965, Henry Hodge and Mac, on separate occasions, came to visit me in Kenfig Hill. I took them to my grandparents' house, which had no inside toilet or bathroom, and to public houses that closed only in the event of no customer present wishing to purchase alcoholic beverages. Pubs had just officially opened on Sundays, and legitimate drinking on the Sabbath was still very much a novelty worthy of celebration. (Voting for Sunday opening and voting for the election of my Uncle Mostyn as a county councillor were the only two ballots in which I ever participated.)

Each had visited Wales before. Mac had been to Snowdonia on an outward bound course organised by his public school and presumed the whole of Wales to be like the Scottish highlands, where his grandparents had an estate packed with grouse and foxhounds. Henry had once visited Portmeirion, for a week's holiday with his parents, and presumed Wales was a coastal, green desert of grass and wet emptiness with the odd oasis of accommodation for the aristocracy, where sheep-shagging farm labourers tended to the titled toffs' every need and indulged their whims. I took them to nearby coal-mining valleys, which revealed gigantic slag heaps, ribbon-terraced housing, a few working coalmines, dozens of chapels, and scores of men-only pubs accommodating individuals capable of drinking more than forty pints of beer in a single session. Such evidence did much to confirm the succession of tall stories I had narrated about my homeland the previous year. Henry and Mac were more than a little embarrassing, insisting on hailing any man serving behind the bar as 'landlord' and ordering unheard-of cocktails in posh BBC voices.

Although technically outside the rugby season, the beginning of September invariably lured vigorous training sessions to take place on various bits of waste ground. The outcome of these, the potential they showed and the prospects of the national Welsh team in the forthcoming season were the subjects of endless volatile discussions. Kenfig Hill is in the dead centre of that relatively small area of Wales (approximately 1,000 square miles and known as 'the valleys') from which the entire Welsh team is invariably picked. Its population lives and breathes rugby while drinking vast quantities of draught beer, both to slake their coal-dust thirsts and get blind pissed. This hedonistic enthusiasm and obsession took Henry and Mac by surprise. They were genuine rugby fans, but on the bases of their respective experiences in England and Scotland, had presumed rugby to be a universal upper-class disciplined sport nurtured in whatever prestigious fee paying schools might be around. The working class, as far as my two friends were concerned, played football, wherever they were.

I began to be able to see Wales through non-

Welsh eyes. Those who had been to the valleys likened the country to the industrial north of England – full of tough, gritty, hard-working, hard-drinking, heavily accented (therefore, inarticulate), friendly, promiscuous, no-nonsense, union-card bearing Labour voters. Visitors to other parts thought the Welsh to be teetotal, xenophobic, indolent, idle, puritanical, foreign (therefore, inarticulate), perverted yokels, who hated but aspired to be English. Those who had spent time in both parts (or neither part) were confused and had no idea what was happening.

As a result, I became aware, for the first time, of a north–south divide. It is not strictly that, but there was certainly a historical post-industrialisation divide between the rural, Welsh-speaking north, mid, and west of Wales and the industrial, English-speaking and international socialist south-east.

During my following two years as an Oxford undergraduate, although I did not (couldn't) lose my Welsh accent, I felt less and less Welsh and lost interest in rugby and Wales. Whether it was north or south, it was all too parochial, restricting, narrow-minded, and trivial. I thought I was part of a bigger world, a world of diverse cultures, races, and religions; a world of drugs other than alcohol, music other than hymns, freedom, free love, and uninhibited self-expression; a world I could help improve by demonstrating against racism, homophobia, and American warmongering and doing my bit spreading the word and the weed.

I fell in love with Oxford's biggest catch – Latvian beauty Ilze Kadegis. Surprisingly, she fell in love with me, and we lived together in 1960s oblivion. During late December of 1967, Ilze and I were married at my parents' local Welsh Congregational chapel. To this day, I have no idea why we took this extraordinary step. We did not intend having children; we had no money; Ilze was destined to become a poorly paid primary schoolteacher; and I was destined for goodness knew what. We took a one-night honeymoon at a bed-and-breakfast establishment in Ogmore-by-Sea, one of just a handful of nights spent in Wales since September 1965.

After graduating, I soon got bored with teaching in London and missed the non-working environment of university life. I wanted to go back. My degree in nuclear physics was good enough to do postgraduate work, but I wanted to study humanities rather than how to blow up large chunks of the world. I applied to Oxford and was accepted to do a diploma in the history and philosophy of science. There was a problem with respect to how my diploma course would be financed. In those days there were two main grant giving bodies funding postgraduate study: the Department of Education and the Science Research Council. The former limited its grants to graduates in non-scientific subjects while the latter would only fund students undertaking research degrees in the pure sciences. These regulations precluded my philosophy of science studies being funded by either body. A thick publication gave a complete list of organisations that funded postgraduate study and the conditions under which they did so. I scoured through this book and discovered the Thomas and Elizabeth Williams Scholarship, which was restricted to those applicants who lived in a small area of Wales, which included Kenfig Hill. My mother's brother, Uncle Mostyn, was then chairman of Glamorgan County Council, an organisation not particularly averse to literal nepotism. I approached him about the possibility of applying for the Thomas and Elizabeth Williams Scholarship, and he arranged for me to be interviewed by the trustees. They agreed to pay all course fees and awarded me a maintenance grant.

Wales had come to my rescue, but I bit the hand that fed me by abandoning my studies and deciding to pursue the career of a drug smuggler.

# 6

# WATER, METAL, AND A BAR IN MALLORCA

THE CONCEPT OF a prostitute was my first abstraction of sex symbolism, and a Kenfig Hill upbringing more than ensured my dealings with prostitutes remained on the abstract level. As a result, the loss of my virginity and other initial real sex encounters were enshrined in a miasma of embarrassment, incompetence, and guilt. The peak of my fertility had coincided with the trough of my sexual inadequacy.

It was 1963, and King's College, University of London, had invited me to be interviewed for a place to read physics. Physics was still coming easily to me, and the interview presented me with no worries. My mind was more concerned with visiting Soho; the sound of the name had always excited me.

After a four-hour train journey terminating at Paddington, I bought a tourist map, caught a tube to the Strand, and dealt with my interview at

King's College. I worked out which underground stations were close to Soho Square and killed time so that I would arrive there by nightfall. I walked down Frith Street and Greek Street. I could not believe it. The place really was like I had imagined it would be. There were strip clubs and prostitutes everywhere. I had never seen either before. I saw the clubs I had read about in the *Melody Maker* and the *New Musical Express*: the Two I's, the Marquee, the Flamingo, and Ronnie Scott's. My heart was thumping with anticipation as I walked down Dean Street and turned into St Anne's Court. The name on the flat's doorbell was Lulu. She was the sexiest girl I had ever seen and asked if I wanted to spend some time with her. I explained I did not have much money. She said not to worry. I told her my name was Deke Rivers (the name of the character Elvis played in *Loving You*). Ten minutes later, I had parted with everything I had – £2 8s. She gave me just a little of what she had, but it was more than enough. I had been blessed with the experience of conscience-free, sweet and powerful sex.

Later that night, skint, I strolled past Lulu's quarters again. A sad looking older person walked anxiously into them. A quarter of an hour later, he emerged full of the joys of life. I did not feel jealous. I was aware I did not feel jealous. Lulu then walked out, stared straight into my eyes without the merest hint or glint of recognition, and strode away. I was very aware of not feeling the least bit hurt.

Therefore, a beautiful woman (who forgot me before my pants were dry) taught me that jealousy was no more than a controllable attitude, that it was insane to get offended by anyone not trying to cause offence, and that sex should be an intensely joyous Big Bang. In those days, the evils I most hated were the capitalist work ethic, racism, war, homophobia, and Americans in Vietnam. I now had one more to add to the list – the social stigmatisation of prostitutes. Given prostitutes were doling out lots of care, why were they being shunned and reviled by the community? Given they were promoting understanding, and spiritual correction, why were they being revered less than nuns? Where is the respect? Why weren't there any around Kenfig Hill? I just had to get away from Wales and start living.

I walked to Hyde Park, then to Paddington and caught the 2 o'clock 'milk train' back to Bridgend.

Looking back, I never managed to stray very far from Welsh connections. Invariably, these were in the most unusual, unexpected and unlikely places.

During 1984 while visiting Bangkok, I was intrigued to read a sub-headline: 'Wales Hopes

On Henry Morgan's trail, Jamaica

My Welsh school motto on a school in Patagonia

Buried home from home

A Welsh Tea Room and Museum in a South American town

The stunning scenery off the southernmost tip of Chile

Rob Brydon with the much missed Stuart Cable

Stuart's signature in the Prince of Wales, Kenfig

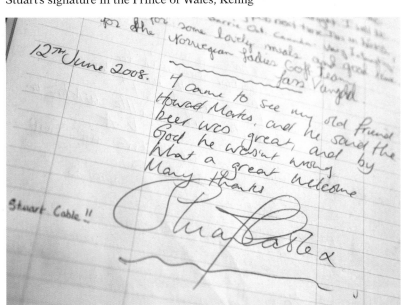

12TH June 2008.

I came to see my old friend Howard Marks. and he said the beer was great, and by God he wasn't wrong What a great welcome Many thanks

Stuart Cable !!

A reflective pint in the Prince of Wales, Wales's most haunted pub

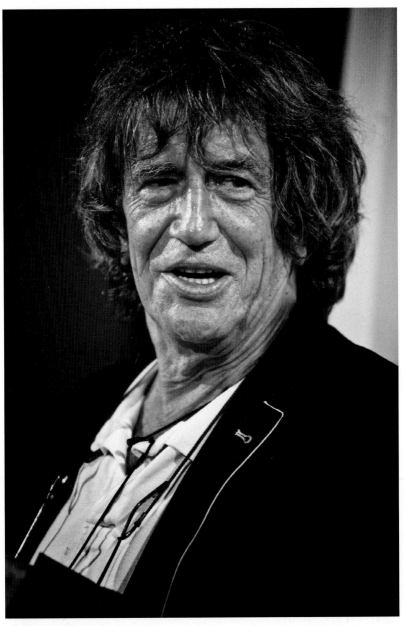

At Gŵyl Arall Literary Festival, Caernarfon, a bilingual gig for me

Above my home village, Kenfig Hill, both rural and industrial

Kenfig Nature Reserve, which my Uncle Mostyn played a large part in securing

Sharing a joke in the hills above my birthplace

I like to get back to the house where I was born as often as possible

In the living room

My best mate Marty; we were pushed around Kenfig in prams together as babies

At an alternative Ryder Cup Golf event, run by GLC – my golf was certainly alternative

With some of the SFA boys at the golf

On location filming *Mr Nice* in the Rhondda

With my son Patrick and daughter Francesca at the premier of *Mr Nice* in Cardiff

Me and the only one who could have been me in a film

to Export its Water' in the *Bangkok Post*. The article explained how the Welsh Water Authority was attempting to sell some of its vast and never-ending supply of freshwater. Storage tanks and facilities would be available in south Wales at Milford Haven, Britain's largest natural harbour and oil importing port. Oil tankers would be bulk-loaded with freshwater piped from the harbour's storage tanks. Many countries were short of water, and this proposal, the article concluded, made a lot more sense than the recently aborted attempt to tow icebergs from the Arctic.

I had a strong urge to get involved in this business. I do not know why, and I did not know how. Drinkbridge, the name of my recently formed wine company, would be a remarkably appropriate name for such a business. One of the keys to business success is to pretend to be doing what one ultimately wants to do. I decided to present myself to the Welsh Water Board as the man who could buy their billions of gallons of surplus water. First, I would need to learn all I could about the subject. That would not be hard: I would read books and employ a researcher. I would also need some credentials: name cards, Drinkbridge company notepaper that did not have grapes and bottles of wine all over it, and a bank account. I had intended to visit Hong Kong before returning to Europe, and it would be an easy matter to sort all that out when there.

The offices of the Welsh Water Authority were just a few hours' drive from Kenfig Hill. I had spent a week reading all there was to know about the bulk transport of water and had made an appointment to see Roy Webborn, the authority's assistant director of finance. I told him I represented a syndicate of Far Eastern businessmen who were interested in purchasing giant tanker loads of water and taking it to Saudi Arabia. Webborn explained that Welsh Water was not yet available for bulk export (although there was plenty of it in the hills) and oil tankers were leaving Milford Haven carrying nothing but seawater ballast. If any business interest was prepared to pay for the installation of bulk freshwater loading facilities at Milford Haven, the Welsh Water Authority would pay for the pipes to take the water there from the hills and sell it cheaply. I said I would see what I could do. He gave me a stack of laboratory test reports and impressive multilingual, multi-coloured brochures.

One of my Bangkok contacts was financing the research of making paper from rice husks and currently submitting the proposal to a joint Saudi/Thai business consortium headed by Sheikh Abdularaman A Alraji, who, according to the *Guinness Book of Records*, was the richest man in the world. If the committee liked the proposal, the Saudis would build a rice husk paper mill in Thailand. I told my friend about the tanker project, and he offered to submit the Welsh water proposal for similar consideration if I could get it together immediately. I had all the documents with me in Bangkok. They were in my briefcase ready to impress any official who wanted to open it. With some concentrated effort, I typed a feasibility report, which was little more than a re-write of the Welsh Water Authority's bumf coupled with some bits and pieces and pasted on to Drinkbridge Hong Kong Limited notepaper. The secretarial services at the Oriental Hotel made the report presentable. Two days later it was completed and I officially submitted the report. It even got a mention in the March 1984 issue of *Tatler*.

Nothing actually came of the plan, but I continued to use my involvement as an excuse to be out east. On one occasion a year or so later, I had gone through passport control at Heathrow's Terminal 3 and was about to enter the pre-boarding room for PIA's flight to Karachi when I was stopped by a policeman in plain clothes.

"We're just having a word with people going out east, sir. Is Karachi your destination or somewhere else in Pakistan?"

"I'm meeting someone in Karachi."

"A business meeting, sir?"

"Yes."

"May I ask, what is your business, sir?"

"I sell water."

"Water?"

"Yes, water. Welsh water, actually."

"Big demand for that in Pakistan, is there, sir?"

"Not that I'm aware of. However, there is a demand for it in nearby Saudi Arabia, and I am meeting Sheikh Abdularaman A Alraji in the Karachi Sheraton. The Sheikh has several businesses in Pakistan. I usually meet him there."

"May I see your passport, sir? Mr Marks, I see you have visited Karachi quite a few times in recent weeks. Bangkok, too. The Sheikh likes to meet you there as well?"

"The company I work for is based in Hong Kong. Flights from Hong Kong to Karachi usually transit through Bangkok. I often take advantage of the opportunity to stay a couple of days in Thailand."

"Thank you, Mr Marks. Enjoy your flight. Sell plenty of water."

I did not know it at the time, but I had been recognised and questioned by one of Her Majesty's Customs and Excise investigative branch officers. They were onto me. They would follow me for a long, long time.

At the beginning of 1988, in my capacity as a travel agent (I was joint owner of Hong Kong International Travel Centre, the largest Far East travel agency in the UK), I visited Taiwan to see some senior representatives of the country's airline, China Airlines. We met at a bar named Hsaling, which was very popular with western visitors. At the end of the meeting, three New Zealand men squeezed in next to me to occupy the two seats vacated. I was drinking whisky and water in separate glasses. Through clumsiness, I knocked over the glass of water onto the lap of one of my new companions. I apologised profusely.

"Are you Welsh?" he asked, brushing off small pools of water.

"Yes, I am."

*"Ydych chi'n siarad Cymraeg?"*

*"Odw."*

"Roy Middleton. Pleased to meet you."

"Howard Marks. Sorry about the water."

"Don't worry. Not Welsh water by any chance, is it?"

"I shouldn't think so, Roy. Mind, a few years ago I was trying to ship the stuff from Wales to the east myself. Maybe someone stole my idea."

"Is that your business then, Howard? Water?"

"No, I'm just a humble travel agent these days,

but I used to dabble a bit in all sorts of trades. What about you? Don't tell me you're a water man."

"No way. I left Wales for New Zealand to get away from the wet. Now, I work for the New Zealand government. Sounds very grand, but all I do is interview Taiwanese who want to emigrate to New Zealand."

"What type do they have to be?"

"Filthy rich, basically. However, here that is quite a broad spectrum. We have immigrated university professors, nuclear research physicists, as well as top industrialists. It is a lot of interviews, but the pay's good. And there's no end of profitable sidelines."

"Like what?"

"Well, the people who want us to grant them New Zealand nationality treat us like bloody gods. They agree to whatever we ask. We can dictate to them what they should invest in when they come to New Zealand, where they should live, and what business they should open. You can imagine there is quite a crowd of New Zealanders with plenty of suggestions. Putting a few of them forward can produce healthy kickbacks for yours truly. We also tell them which hotels to stay in before they settle, even how to travel there. That's all left to us."

"Do you have a good travel agent?"

"I wonder why you're asking, Howard. We don't actually have a regular travel agent. If your prices are competitive, I would love to give a fellow Welshman the business. Come to think of it, why don't you try to persuade some Taiwanese to set up a factory or two in Wales, Howard? That would bring some employment to the area. Look how many Japanese factories there are in Wales. The Taiwanese are the new Japanese and want to get themselves in everywhere to make lots of money."

"Why aren't they in Wales already?"

"Because, Howard, no Welshman has presented the Taiwanese with a proposal embodying attractive terms: tax incentives, residency, and long term naturalisation prospects. Why don't you become the first person to set up a Taiwanese plant in Wales?"

"How do I find Taiwanese likely to be attracted by such a proposal?"

"I see about twenty every day."

Every seven years past members of Balliol College are invited to a reunion of their contemporaries. I had graduated in 1967 but had ignored the invitations of 1974 and 1981. I accepted the June 1988 invitation. It was strange to stroll through Balliol's front quadrangle once again. My contemporaries had changed very little in twenty years, and old friendships and alliances were quickly rekindled. There seemed to be no disapproval of my exploits in the hashish smuggling trade, just interest and polite curiosity. One of my Oxford contemporaries, a fellow Welshman named Peter Gibbins, had become a very successful academic. During vacations, he ran seminars on information technology aimed at managerial audiences from all parts of the world. We talked about Taiwan and the demand there for knowledge of European business practice. Peter asked if I would be able to recruit delegates from Taiwan to attend a seminar series that he would organise and for which he would arrange prestigious academic speakers. It might even be possible to provide accommodation for the Taiwanese delegates at student college rooms in Balliol. With Roy's help, I obtained China Metal's tentative agreement to open a factory in south Wales. A number of industrial managers expressed interested in attending seminars in Oxford. But before things could really take off, the authorities had other ideas and law triumphed over business.

Between late 1982 and early 1984, the Inland Revenue targeted me, and my accountant advised me to become a foreign resident. Spain seemed a sensible choice, so I flew to Palma de Mallorca and stayed at a friend's flat in Magaluf while looking for a suitable place to live. The immediate vicinity fulfilled all one's nightmares about package holidays. The streets were packed with screaming British football hooligans. Pubs with names such as London Pride, Rovers' Return, Benny Hill, and Princess Di, emptied lager louts into a bewildering array of discotheques, souvenir stalls, and fish and chip shops. Strangely enough, there were very few street fights. A similar alcoholic and boisterous mass thronging a British street would very quickly turn into a riot. The holidaymakers looked happy. Even paradise could not compete with guaranteed sunshine, ubiquitous promiscuity, and non-stop drinking. I rented a car and had a look around the island. Within minutes, the stench of booze and vomit was replaced by sweet perfumes of cherry and almond blossoms. Most of Mallorca is deserted and beautifully tranquil. The highest mountain is taller than any in the British Isles. At its foot live people who have never seen the sea, thirty miles away. Small villages hang off hills and provide accommodation for some of the world's greatest artists, musicians, and writers. The city of Palma is a delightful mixture of medieval Italian and Moorish architecture. People smoked hash in the street. The weather was perfect.

In the fifteenth century, a little Mallorquian

settlement named Es Vinyet was famous for its density of vines. A plague destroyed them, and Es Vinyet disappeared for a few hundred years until it was renamed and repopulated by a few farmers at the beginning of the last century. Its new name was La Vileta. Because of the impossibility of building any closer to Palma's city walls, La Vileta attracted Mallorquians who were seeking jobs in the city. It changed from a rural area to a dormitory for Palma's carpenters and stonemasons. These craftsmen utilised their considerable skills in customising their own homes and communal buildings. La Vileta's architecture is far from uniform, and it has many peculiar buildings. I had bought one of them, a three-floored, 150-year-old house with stone walls a few feet thick, and five enormous palm trees struggling to share a small garden. La Vileta has plenty of bars, and these, like most bars in Spain, serve perfectly adequate food.

There is, however, only one actual restaurant in La Vileta, named appropriately enough, Restaurante La Vileta. It was owned and successfully run by Bob Edwardes, a Welshman hailing from Ogmore-by-sea. Naturally, we were drawn to each other's company.

Bob explained that there were several Welsh people living in Mallorca. There was even a Welsh piano bar in the north of the island, Palma's most exclusive hotel was named Casa Gales, and Air Wales provided regular flights to and from Cardiff. According to Bob, the Spanish had an enormous respect and fondness for the Welsh, which stemmed from the Spanish Civil War, when Wales joined the country's unsuccessful fight against the fascists. In Deja, the home of Robert Graves, there were families who were bilingual in Welsh and Mallorquian, the local Catalan dialect.

Bob became one of the best friends anyone could wish to have. When I was arrested four years later and extradited to the United States, Bob was the first person to visit me in prison and wrote to me on a regular basis for the next eight years.

It is, perhaps, ironic that in July 1988, my last taste of freedom before being arrested the following morning was a few pints of beer at Taffy's Bar in Magaluf.

# 7

# BILLY THE KID, GANGSTERS, AND PIRATES

ALL THOSE STRANDS, all the disjointed, hidden Welsh roots, the connections, the accidents of time and geography lay dormant until that random conversation with an American gangster called Tee Bone in one of his country's most notorious prisons. Back home, and free again, I started to look further, deeper into my Welshness in a way I had not done before.

Shortly after my father's death in October 1996, and one month after the publication of *Mr Nice* I decided to search the attic. It was my bedroom when I was a teenager and it had generally served as a depository for all things not needing instant access by my parents. I rummaged through the bookshelves and cabin trunks and sifted through mounds of old school exercise books, cuttings from do-it-yourself magazines, and yellowing documents that once held significance for some now forgotten ancestor. I knew so little about my ancestry but now, for the first time in my life, I wanted to learn more. I had better start soon before all my family passed away.

The oldest surviving member of my maternal family was my Grandpa Ben's sister, Afon Wen – which means white river and is almost never used as a personal name for anyone. She was as precious as the roughest of diamonds. Much to her dismay, she now lived in an old people's home couched between Kenfig and Kenfig Hill, between the M4 and the sewage farm, which she referred to as the perfume factory. By the strangest of coincidences, Afon Wen was also the name of the deep-sea salvage tug that, during December 1979, landed fifteen tons of the finest Colombian marijuana on the western Scottish island of Kerrera. I was accused of masterminding the importation but after a nine-week trial was cleared of the charge by an Old Bailey jury, having persuaded them I was a spy.

Although it was just a bizarre coincidence, I feel convinced that if Her Majesty's Customs and Excise had been aware that the offending boat had the same very unusual name as my great aunt, my acquittal would never have happened.

I walked into the home and found Aunt Afon Wen's room.

"Auntie 'Fon, is there anyone famous in our family on Mam's side?"

"I don't think so at all, unless we count you, of course. If they weren't down the pits digging coal for the bloody English, they were writing poetry. None of them actually became famous except Dyfnallt Owen, who was a great uncle of Nana Jones, your mother's mother. He became an archdruid of Wales. A bit of a wizard, too, according to Nana Jones, who had no end of stories about him boiling up magical potions and doing all sorts of tricks with them, tricks he had learnt from his mother's father, Dafydd Rhys Williams, a brother or first cousin of none other than Edward Williams, better known as Iolo Morganwg."

"Well, he's definitely famous Auntie 'Fon. I've heard of him."

"I'm sure, but it's pushing it a bit to say he's part of the family, Howard *bach*. He's a very distant relation, if any at all. Mind, I'm not surprised you have heard of him. He was a bloody opium addict. Clever though, by all accounts. They say Iolo invented the eisteddfod. That's how Dyfnallt Owen became its archdruid. It's always been the same, hasn't it, Howard *bach*? It's who you know not what you know. Dyfnallt's grandfather, William Owen, was quite famous in his time. Well, infamous would be a better way of describing him, as it would with you. They say he was the greatest ever Welsh smuggler, not drugs mind. He was executed in Carmarthen. I think he wrote an autobiography, too. They discovered it quite recently. Now that's a coincidence, isn't it?"

My aunt might not have all the facts right, but I later found out the previously unknown autobiography of William Owen had turned up in 1982. After a few successful smuggling runs between Wales and the Isle of Man, Owen worked in South America for a well-armed worldwide smuggler named 'The Terrible'. Owen's sexual liaisons resulted in illegitimate children of all colours, and his chronicle of scams, acquittals, and debauchery would put any modern-day smuggler or playboy to shame.

"This gets better and better, Auntie 'Fon. Any others?"

"Well there's my mother's half-brother, Madoc. I can't go into it too much. I think there was a bit of incest going on. There was more of that in those days. But he gave me my name, Afon Wen, which I've never been keen on. Mind, it's a good name for a squaw, don't you think? Madoc always claimed he was a Red Indian brought up in a wigwam with totem poles outside it. And he thought he was a direct descendant of a Welsh prince who was also the first of the Incas. He used to say the Incas were his cousins. He wanted to go to Patagonia and join the Welsh colony there, like a lot of people from the valleys did. They got on very well with the Red Indians, by all accounts. Madoc got jealous because he had always felt he belonged on the other side of the Atlantic with the Red Indians and their wigwams. He never made it, though. He got killed by lightning."

The oldest surviving member of my paternal family was my grandfather's eldest sister, Katie Marks. She was ninety and lived in her own flat in Kenfig Hill. I had never known her very well and hadn't seen her for about fifteen years.

"Hello Howard *bach*. Lovely to see you after all these years. You must be glad to be back from America. What are you doing with yourself these days?"

"Writing and doing shows. I've turned over a new leaf."

"That's right, Howard *bach*, put the past behind you."

"Well, actually, Auntie Katie, it's the past I wanted to talk to you about."

"Oh dear! How can I help?"

"Who was my grandfather Tudor's father?"

"Dafydd Marks. He owned half of Kenfig Hill."

"And who was his father? Was that Patrick Marks?"

"That's right. Patrick Marks, a very religious

man in the end. He is buried up the road in Siloam Chapel, Cefn Cribbwr."

"And his father? Who was he?"

"Well, that's when it does get a bit confusing. It seems that Patrick changed his name from McCarty to Marks."

"Why?"

"There are three theories. One was to inherit a lot of money from a German Jewish family called Marks who worked the coalmines round by here. Another was to hide himself because he had made a lot of money abroad in a way he shouldn't have, and the foreign police were after him. The third theory, and this is the one I think is true, was to get rid of the bad name and reputation of his relative, who was Billy the Kid, of course. Patrick's father, who was also called Patrick, was Billy the Kid's father as well, but with another woman."

"This is incredible. My great-great-grandfather was Billy the Kid's brother."

"Half-brother I think, isn't it? But there's more, Howard *bach*, lots more. The McCartys were also in Jesse James's gang and got together with Butch Cassidy and the Sundance Kid in Patagonia, the headquarters of all the Irish and Welsh cowboys in those days. Apparently, Patrick learned Welsh there. Anyway, after years out in South America, he decided to come and live here in south Wales under another name. Not that changing his name did Patrick much good, mind. His son, your great-grandfather Dafydd's brother, Willie Bevan Marks, became a notorious Chicago gangster. He was Bugs Moran's first lieutenant. I wasn't a bit surprised you became a famous smuggler, not a bit."

"Is this true, Auntie Katie?"

"Every word. Why do you think your grandfather Tudor's brother, Tommy, called all his children something Bevan Marks, including the girls? He was hoping Willie would leave them his money."

"Did he?"

"Not a penny."

I had to check the veracity of this and called into Kenfig Hill's library to surf the net.

Billy the Kid was born in 1861 in New York to Patrick and Catherine McCarty and named William Henry McCarty. A few years later, Patrick left Catherine, who married William Antrim and died when young Billy was thirteen. Billy became an outlaw, teaming up with Welshman Jesse Evans, the leader of a gang of rustlers called 'The Boys'. To avoid capture, Billy changed his name to William H Bonney. That is as far as I got. It was more than enough to convince me Auntie Katie was right.

At the beginning of prohibition, Willie Marks joined Dean O'Bannion's North Side Gang of Chicago and became best friends with fellow gang member George 'Bugs' Moran, who later became leader of the gang and made Willie Marks second in command. His duties included the management of all the gang's South American interests. Willie Marks narrowly missed being murdered by Al Capone in the St Valentine's Day massacre but was later fatally machine-gunned by Al Capone's James 'Fur' Sammons, a well-known psychotic who was convicted of the rape, mutilation, and murder of an 11-year-old schoolgirl. Willie Marks is buried in Woodlawn Cemetery in Forest Park, Illinois.

I rummaged around the attic again. Dozens of boxes contained various belongings of mine from days gone by – old school exercise and textbooks, chemistry and Meccano sets, unopened wedding presents from my 1967 marriage to Ilze, rock and psychedelic posters, hundreds of letters, and reams of pretentious philosophical writing from the days when I thought my only possible career was as an academic. One box had been sent from the United States federal penitentiary, Terre Haute. It had lain there unopened and contained all the photographs, books, and letters that had been sent to me during my years as a prisoner but which the prison authorities had judged to be detrimental to maintaining good order in the prison. One was a photograph of my son when he was aged two taking his first swim. It had not been allowed to pass into my hands because he was not wearing a swimming costume. There were several inoffensive books on drugs, crime, sex, and politics, some of which contained dedications to me handwritten by the authors. These were automatically banned: books had to be sent to the prison in virgin condition direct from the publishers. Unsurprisingly, my attention focused on a book entitled *Madoc – The Legend of the Welsh Discovery of America*. The author, Gwyn A Williams, had dedicated it to me. An envelope of articles and pamphlets on the same subject peeped out from inside the book. I settled down to read, highlighting and scribbling frantically.

Prince Madoc, the illegitimate son of Welsh king Owain the Great, had become disillusioned with royal life. In 1170, he and some of his friends set sail from Abergele, currently a small village and large caravan park near Colwyn Bay, and landed in Alabama. Both Abergele and Fort Morgan, Mobile, Alabama, carry plaques to Madoc's memory. Leaving behind a small group, Madoc returned to Wales with tales of the warm, luscious land he had found. He picked up supplies and more ships full of like-minded fellow compatriots and was never seen again. One pamphlet claimed that Madoc, on his second visit, landed and settled in Mexico. There were several Welsh words in the Aztec language resulting from contact between the Mexicans and the Welsh settlers. One of these was the name of a strange new bird, the penguin, the Welsh for 'white head'. I took a break from my research and suddenly realised that they had black heads. My heart fell. I had been reading a complete load of nonsense. I drifted asleep, weary and depressed.

I woke up with a crystal-clear mind. The penguin problem alone had provoked my doubt about the existence of Welsh Native Americans. The rest made perfect sense. Back on-line, I searched for 'white-headed penguins' and came across the Great Auk (*Pinguinus impennis*), a big, northern hemisphere penguin with a dominant white patch on its head. Great Auks, although extinct for over 150 years, lived in great numbers on islands off Britain, Iceland, and Greenland and were sources of food and down, especially for mariners crossing the Atlantic. Almost all birds had black heads, so the Great Auk could be distinguished by its white crown. When the Welsh settlers came across southern hemisphere penguins, the striking similarity in shape between those and the Great Auks resulted in the same name (penguin) being used for both. I felt relieved. Great aunt Afon Wen's account of

Native American Indians was no flight of fancy. It was confirmed in works of scholarship. Could she also have been right about the Incas?

In 1908, the Reverend John H Parry of the University of Durham published *Manco Capac The First Inca of Peru, Being a Critical Inquiry into the Pretensions concerning the Discovery of America by Prince Madawg Ap Owen Gwynedd with Reflections upon the Final Discovery of that Continent, by Christopher Columbus; and upon some of the Historical Antiquities of America,* which argued that Madoc became known as Manco Capac, the first Inca of Peru. Manco Capac's appearance on the shores of Peru occurred a few weeks after Madoc's disappearance from Wales. Mama Ocello (a corruption of *Mama Uchel*) was at his side. The couple were considered the progenitors of the Incas. Auntie 'Fon, like Auntie Katie, was right.

It was autumn 2002, and I realised I would never escape from the grief of my mother having recently died, far from peacefully, in my and my sister's arms. I might become familiar with the loss, but I would not recover from it. For a while, life became frighteningly empty and sickeningly pointless. My capacity to concentrate evaporated, childhood recall filled my memory, and I looked forward to nothing. It began to seem particularly silly to carry on with the search for my ancestry when I had just lost the most precious part of it.

I had been using the attic in the same way as my parents had – a store for stuff I didn't need immediately. Eclectic bric-a-brac and pamphlets still littered the bookshelves and overflowed from cardboard boxes and suitcases. Would it ever be sensibly sorted and classified or would it just wait until irrelevant to anyone left alive and end up in a skip? I came across a tin cabin trunk stuffed full of *National Geographic* magazines, maps, charts, and guidebooks to countries all over the world and began filing into one box anything relating to South America. There were ashtrays inlaid with moth wings from Brazil, ceramic figurines from Peru, a marble statuette of Christ of the Andes, a Uruguayan basket made from the carapace of an armadillo, guide booklets to Inca, Aztec, and Mayan monuments, and cheap souvenirs from most of the continent's capitals. My obsession with Welsh and South American matters returned in full force as butterflies started dancing in my guts. I saw a small battered brown leather wallet, opened it and found a folded envelope. On the back of the envelope was written 'Patrick McCarty'. Inside was a small and faded black-and-white photograph of a narrow channel of rough sea bordered with sharp pointed pencil mountains. On the back was written 'Patagonia', the seeming home at various times of ancestors on both sides of my family. I didn't need any more messages, signs, or coincidences. I made plans to visit Patagonia. My ancestry quest had returned with a vengeance.

# 8

# GAUCHOS,
# TEA ROOMS, AND GLACIERS

I FLEW VIA Buenos Aires to Trelew in the Chubut Valley. A statue of a giant penguin with a black head dominated the arrivals hall. Murals of dolphins, sea lions, and whales covered the walls. Signs warned against the dangers of bringing in any animals, foodstuffs, or other carriers of viruses or bacteria into Patagonia, the world's biggest complex of nature reserves and wildlife sanctuaries. I joined passengers boarding a public bus destined for Puerto Madryn, where the Welsh first landed over 150 years ago. For fifty body-shaking miles, the bus bounced on a straight and empty road spearing through thousands of square miles of flat military green thorn scrub. The sea magically sprang into view, and one could see the tops of buildings nestling in a cove on the coast. A long pier with a massive cruise ship on each side stretched out into the ocean. Shops by the harbour sold motor boats, kayaks, canoes, jet skis, windsurfer boards, and deep-sea fishing and diving gear. Puerto Madryn was not a typical Welsh village; it was a thriving North American styled water sports resort and marina.

Somewhat disappointed, I got off the bus, located a suitable hotel, and went for a walk into the town looking for anything Welsh. Eventually, I came across streets named Matthews, Roberts, Humphreys, and Love Jones Parry. Relieved, I walked down Love Jones Parry until I came back to the promenade. A large monument, designed in 1965 by Luis Perlotti, the famous Argentinean sculptor, commemorated the centenary of the Welsh landing in Punta Cuevas. I took a cab there. Strolling along the shore, I was suddenly confronted by a statue of a Native American perched on top of a pile of old stones. He was holding a bow in one hand and shielding his eyes from the sun with another. A notice board stated that this was 'El Indio', another Luis Perlotti statue marking the gratitude of the Welsh to the native Tehuelche people, whose shared expertise ensured their survival. Some caves with boarded openings lay nearby. I walked up to another notice, which stated that the Welsh had landed here and had lived in these caves.

The Welsh adventurers found freshwater near the estuary of the Chubut river and set up smallholdings and a fishing community at a place now named Trerawson, known simply as Rawson. The government of Argentina was not simply being generous in offering the Welsh a large chunk of their land. To create such a colony also satisfied Argentinean interests. The government needed to strengthen its presence in the area to fight against threats from Chile and from England because of the Falklands/Malvinas dispute. England was the common enemy of Argentina and Wales. The Argentinean minister of the interior, Dr Rawson, eased matters by keenly supporting the formation of a Welsh colony and giving his name to the country's first Welsh settlement. Used to working in mines, the Welsh found farming difficult. Unaware of the different seasons in the southern hemisphere, they sowed crops in autumn instead of spring and had to face one failure after another. They were saved from starvation by a Tehuelche Indian tribe who set up camp close by, thereby beginning an astonishing and friendly relationship with the Welsh settlers, teaching them how to handle cattle, ride horses, and hunt. They bartered meat and pelts for bread and butter and even staged their own sports fixtures. The Welsh won the shooting; the Tehuelche won the equestrian events. The close bond established between them has held until the present day.

Nevertheless, the first few years were tough

for the settlers, and the population fell. Over the years, the Welsh introduced irrigation and were eventually able to export wheat. The population increased. Remembering their debt, the Welsh took abandoned Tehuelche children and orphans into their care and taught them Welsh. Intermarriage with local Spanish speakers was encouraged, provided all spoke Welsh.

The heart of the existing Welsh community was a bit further away at Gaiman. There was a monopoly of Welsh street names, dusty rows of flinty Welsh cottages, hacienda-style houses, stern-looking chapels and more tea houses than there are in all of Wales. I parked the car in Avenida Jones, where Welsh teachers opened Patagonia's first and still active secondary school. The school motto was chiselled above the entrance: *Nid Byd, Byd Heb Wybodaeth*, precisely the same motto as the Garw Grammar School, which I had attended.

A few yards away, a Welsh tea house, *Casa de Te Gales* served afternoon tea. Familiar Welsh paintings and tea towels covered the walls. Welsh arias and the aromas of my childhood drenched the atmosphere. Fine old ladies loaded blue and white gingham clothed tables with munchies and cosy-covered teapots full of proper miners' brew ready to treat the dozens of Argentinean aristocrats who had driven hours to sample the delights of a traditional Welsh high tea. I lost myself in surreal nostalgic reveries and smiled at everyone and chatted to anyone who returned my smile. A young woman wearing a white blouse, sporting both her name, Bronwen Lopez and a prominent Welsh dragon, carried more plates full of Welsh fruit cakes, tarts, spiced breads, jams, and scones to my table.

"*Siarad Cymraeg?*" she asked.

"*Odw,*" I replied, feeling more unreal.

Bronwen was delighted to meet someone from Wales and introduced me to her fellow waitresses, Dolores Jones and Claudia Williams, great-great-granddaughters of two of the passengers on the *Mimosa*, the ship on which the Welsh had sailed across the Atlantic. We talked at length about Wales and I explained my quest to find out whether any McCartys had ever lived in the Chubut Valley. They suggested I visit the keeper of the town's museum, Tegai Roberts. Her great-aunt was born during the *Mimosa*'s voyage and her great-grandfather, Lewis Jones, was the first Welsh person to set foot in South America. Trelew was named after him. She would be able to help.

Tegai Roberts is the older stateswoman of Welsh and no Welsh person would ever be forgiven for visiting Gaiman and not paying her due homage. With overpowering grace, she welcomed me to the museum in Spanish. I answered in

Welsh, and her eyes sparkled. I asked if she had a list of the names of the *Mimosa* passengers and from where in Wales they came. She knew of no McCartys or old stories of any Irishmen having come here but thought it well within the bounds of possibility.

I went back to Trelew to have a drink at the Touring Club Hotel, where anyone who matters today hangs out and where all the bad guys hung out a hundred years ago. In 1901, Butch Cassidy and the Sundance Kid fled to Argentina to pursue a career of ranching. All they wanted was to lead a peaceful life hidden from the world. Their home in Cholilo, at the western end of the Chubut Valley was often the scene of music, dance, and other revelry, well attended and much loved by the dignitaries of the area. To buy supplies and sell produce, they would travel 400 miles to Trelew and stay for long periods in rooms that now form part of the Touring Club Hotel.

The eating and drinking area was a huge cowboy saloon with fans suspended from a high ceiling, newspapers rolled up on sticks, old peeling mirrors, polished light wooden tables and chairs, antiquated but functioning cappuccino machines, and a bar longer than a cricket pitch. Shelves contained hundreds of spirit and wine bottles, beer and cider cans, and black-and-white group photographs lined the walls. I looked at each faded photograph intently. Many carried names of the people pictured. I looked for the name McCarty. And there it was. Rubbing my eyes and cleaning the photograph's frame, I treble-checked. There was no doubt I was reading the name correctly – Patrick McCarty. He and a few of his mates were leaning against a white stone wall and making hand gestures similar to those made by today's hip-hop artists. I could not detect any family likeness, and there was no clue as to where the photograph had been taken. However, this was no coincidence: I had found my great-great-grandfather. I took a snap of the photograph.

A local phone directory lay on the bar. I thumbed through it searching for McCartys. I found three Mac Karthys, and rang them. They insisted they were neither Welsh nor Irish and had no connections with either country. However, one of the Mac Karthys said his father had often talked about an Irishman called Patrick McCarty who had come to live in Gaiman and had learned Welsh at the local school. He was close friends with another guy also learning Welsh, a Chilean called Juan Williams, who was an admiral in the Chilean navy and a hero in the independence war against Spain. He and Patrick were inseparable, apparently, the best of mates. They both left here together at the same time, probably for the same place, Ushuaia, the most southern city in

Patagonia, in fact, in the world. The next day, I caught a flight there, landed in a snowstorm, and took a taxi to the main street, San Martin, a non-stop parade of shops stuffed with world's end souvenirs, penguin paraphernalia, duty-free whisky and cigarettes. The snow eased off. I walked to Volver, an old-fashioned restaurant at the water's edge and reputedly the best Antarctic king crab restaurant in the world. Inside, shelves housing hundreds of old photographs and piles of end-of-the-world bric-a-brac jutted out from walls covered with yellow newspapers. The menu offered crab pâté, crab salad, crab soup, crab pasta, crab goulash, and crab. I ordered crab. Soon afterwards, I was feasting at a plate covered with a crab, its spindly legs spanning over a yard from tip to tip lying on its back. The meat was delicious.

I gazed at the old photographs. Would I strike lucky again? There were no obvious portraits of a Patrick McCarty. While browsing, I noticed some empty boxes labelled 'Fabrica Centolla, Puerto Williams'. I was on to something. I found out Puerto Williams, although in Chile, was just twenty kilometres away on the island of Navarino.

I walked to the expansive harbour, where tour operators were offering trips down the Beagle Channel. A catamaran went via a sea lion colony to Puerto Williams and came back the same day through rocky outcrops housing colonies of cormorants. It was leaving in just over an hour. There were ten other passengers, half of whom were a mixed group of American yachties, returning from a duty-free shopping trip in Ushuaia to boats moored in Puerto Williams and chattering animatedly about prices in voices louder than the catamaran engines.

We rocked and rolled for an hour through choppy sea, passed some thick-necked sea lions shooting out clouds of hot breath to delighted sea lionesses basking on a wreck-strewn beach, and pulled into Puerto Williams. Greeting the catamaran were four youths, each one holding a lead, taking their king crabs for a walk. This was one of the strangest places imaginable. Nothing suggested Puerto Williams had existed for longer than a few decades. It couldn't possibly have had anything to do with either my great-great-grandfather or a nineteenth-century Chilean naval hero. However, walking around I discovered Puerto Williams later developed as a naval base, whose personnel had built the wooden homes I had just seen. It was baptized Puerto Williams in honour of Chilean naval hero Admiral Juan Williams. So there was a connection. This was doing my head in! I needed a drink. Through a clearing in the drizzle, I could see a sunken tugboat connected to the land by a bridge. The tug's top decks had been converted to Club de

Yates Micalvi. I walked into a cosy lounge bar, its crackling wood fire warming and drying groups of yachties, and ordered a very large whisky, which pounded through my temples as I watched the rainstorm turn into a snowstorm and back into a rainstorm. Mists swirled around like ghostly dervishes. The fog lifted. I saw what I had never seen or heard of before, a straight horizontal rainbow. Shrouded in mist, the multi-coloured and spectral carpet played havoc with my understanding of optics. Then I saw something I had seen before, rows of towering granite needles pointing at the sky.

"The Teeth of Navarino. Aren't they just the neatest little pointed hills you've ever seen?" said a nearby American yachtie. I was unable to speak. There was no doubt. They were the spiky hills in the photograph I had found in Kenfig Hill.

A few weeks later, I returned to Puerto Williams but discovered nothing of relevance to my quest. I've researched the matter further in libraries in the United Kingdom and Spain, but still nothing conclusive. The closest I got was reading about an Irishman calling himself Patrick Brendan, befriending a Patagonian Indian, Chief Casimoro. They were such good friends that the Indian chief gave Patrick the Straits of Magellan for nothing. Then Patrick went up and down the straits collecting bird shit from his own land and not letting anyone else have any. He collected tons and tons of it, made millions, and had to scarper across the Atlantic because he got caught up with the fighting between Argentina and Chile over the border.

I would love to prove this was my great-great-grandfather, but I haven't been able to yet.

# 9

# NUMBER NINE, A TANK, AND JACK

IN 1996, WELSHMEN seemed to be dominant in breaking the borders of boredom, particularly in music. For many years, the Welsh had very rarely featured as pioneers of innovative contemporary music. Admittedly, there had been a modest number of Welsh singing successes, such as Ricky Valance, Bonnie Tyler, and Tom Jones, but there had been no ballsy barrier breakers of the calibre of the Stones, Beatles, Sex Pistols, or Oasis. The Manic Street Preachers from Newport broke the impasse. At last, Welsh street culture had an avenue of export. Other bands followed in their wake.

"Could I speak to Howard Marks, please?"

"Speaking."

"It's Emma Broughton from Creation here. You know the Super Furry Animals, a band based in Cardiff?"

"I know of them, for sure, and I've heard a

couple of their tracks, but I don't know them personally."

"Did you know their first album, which is about to be released, has a song about you on it?"

"Fantastic! I had no idea."

"I'll send you a copy of their CD. Let me know if you like it. If you do, we might have a proposition for you."

The CD, a promo copy of *Fuzzy Logic* arrived the next day. The tenth track was called 'Hangin' with Howard Marks'. I loved it.

"I think it's great, Emma."

"Wicked, isn't it?"

"What's the proposition?"

"Well, what inspired them to write the song in the first place was all those false passport pictures of you that some newspapers published when you were released. They want to put them all on the front of their album. Would that be a problem, either from a personal or copyright point of view?"

"Emma, I'd be over the moon if they did that. The pictures were taken in automatic photo booths, so there's no copyright issue."

"Fantastic! And they would like you to come and see them play at the Pontypridd Civic Hall."

I went, of course. The civic hall was packed. I

took my place anonymously and nervously at the back. The concert was first class, an innovative combination of almost every genre I had heard from Status Quo to Zappa and innovative tunes that came from God knows where. The crowd were in raptures as they body-surfed, jumped up and down, and waved their arms in pure joy. I went backstage to meet the band. We got on, we giggled, and we enjoyed the booze and the then novel experience of being the subject of photographers' attention. The Super Furry Animals' debut album was about to be released, as was my autobiography. A few people asked for my autograph, including a tall blond man with a permanent smile, who held out a packet of king-size cigarette papers and a marker pen.

"Can I have your signature, please How?" asked a quiet Welsh voice.

"Sure. What's your name?"

"No, it's your name I want. On these cigarette papers, if that's all right."

"Of course it's all right. I thought perhaps you might want me to dedicate it to somebody."

"How do you mean? Dedicate it?"

"Well, like write 'To Jack' or something."

"Jack who?"

"Jack anybody."

"Fuck Jack. It's for me. I bought these fuckers with my own money."

"Just my signature?"

"Aye, that's it," answered Rhys, looking at me as if I was a simpleton.

I wrote a large signature across the king-sized papers' cardboard covering.

Rhys looked down at the scrawl with disgust.

"I meant every one."

"What do you mean?" I asked.

"Can you please sign every cigarette paper? I'll give Jack some of them." Rhys could not keep it up any longer and started laughing.

"Sorry, How. My name's Rhys." I, too, burst out laughing.

"Good to meet you, Rhys. Where do you live?"

"On Daf Ieuan the drummer's floor until I get a job. I get nervous there, mind. He hits things for a living. Can I ask you something serious?"

"Go on."

"I'm an actor, a bloody good one even when I'm pissed. If they ever make a film of your life, can I play you?"

"Definitely." I meant it.

"It's a deal, Rhys. But you have to keep to it."

"Let's shake on it, How."

Soon afterwards, Rhys starred in the first Welsh drug film, *Twin Town*, then went on to steal the show from Hugh Grant in *Notting Hill* and is now one of the world's most respected actors. We became good friends and entrenched our hell-raising tendencies with an annual drug and drink competition at Glastonbury.

Later the same year (1996), the Super Furry Animals bought a tank and promised me I could drive it at the Reading Festival. The military machine had been converted into a giant techno blaster with a gun barrel modified to fire sliced bread into famine-stricken pockets of the festival crowd.

"Creation Records won't let you drive the tank here. They won't let any of us drive it," said Daf. "Something about it not being insured. Anyway, we're thinking of getting a Spitfire once Creation gets shot of our tank."

"Why are they getting rid of it?" I asked

"Economics I expect, Howard. You know what these record companies are like. Nobody we know can actually drive it. It's too big for most roads. A transporter has to carry it with a special police escort. Parking fees are bad."

I gazed at the tank. Cardiff DJs, The Sacred Grooves, were inside its body, letting loose tidal waves of hammering, honking, and hoofing techno. Frenetic, serious, and beautiful humans were dancing on its roof and all around. The tank had had a shitty life: Northern Ireland, the Falklands, and Bosnia and must have witnessed immeasurable misery, death, and sadness. It had been stuck in trenches, overturned in bloody mud, covered in muddy blood, shot at, given headaches by hand grenades, impounded, and busted. Now God had given it a heart transplant. Gone were the arteries of artillery. A different kind of smoke filled its lungs.

"We're on," said Daf. "Come with us, Howard. You can stand at the back of the stage. The view's great."

Eighty thousand people heaved and swayed to the Furries' rendering of 'Hangin' with Howard Marks'. I hid in the shadows of speakers and scaffolds.

"Now I'd like to introduce Howard Marks," announced Gruff, the lead vocalist.

"He's going to sing his favourite Beatles' song."

They had not warned me about this. They knew I suffered from stage fright. I was cornered. I could slope off, lose my street cred, and be forever mocked and reviled in the valleys of my homeland. Alternatively, I could walk to the front of the stage and sing a Beatles' song with roughly the same result. A few refrains fought each other in my mind, but I could not remember how they started. Then I remembered the Beatles had written a song whose only lyrics were "Number Nine, Number Nine, Number Nine..." I grabbed the microphone, screamed "Number Nine" ninety-nine times, and ambled down to thunderous applause aimed at the Furries' return to centre stage.

Despite the humiliation they risked occasioning me, I developed a great liking for the band and worked with them several times during the years that followed. I did a remix of their anthem ('The Man Don't Give a Fuck'), took confessions from their fans in a confession box erected in the Royal Festival Hall specifically for that purpose (the confessions were transmitted live to a giant screen in the auditorium), and introduced them to their adoring public at the Cardiff International Arena. Through them, I met virtually all the famous Welsh bands at the time, including Catatonia and Gorky's Zygotic Monkey. The Super Furries and I attended each other's performances several times, were interviewed simultaneously on the same radio programmes, and constantly ran into each other at various festivals. Our friendship is very special to me in so many ways.

# DIRTY MONEY, KELLY, AND CABLE

D URING THE 1997 General Election, I was busily campaigning to become a Member of Parliament when the BBC called me and asked if I would be interested in selling them the TV rights to *Mr Nice*. I met Michael Wearing, who as BBC head of serials had supervised several productions, including the new era of costume drama literary adaptations such as *Middlemarch* and *Pride and Prejudice*. Michael and I got on very well with each other, and we signed contracts to produce a six-part series based on *Mr Nice*.

As regards crooks benefiting directly from their crimes, public opinion is consistent: bank robbers should not hang on to the currency they stole, and hit men must not expect to keep their wages if caught. However, opinions vary when people consider whether criminals should benefit indirectly from their offensive behaviour. Could a convicted paedophile write and publish something along the lines of Vladimir Nabokov's *Lolita*? Would Osama Bin Laden, if caught and eventually released, be permitted to work as a paid consultant on an Al Qaeda film? Should criminals be able to publish autobiographical works and sell them? Should gangsters receive a penny for advising directors on how to make a film about the mob? Probably due to having served a long prison sentence and showing no signs of reverting to dope smuggling, I was deemed as having done my time and having settled my debt to society. Accordingly, there was negligible opposition to my writing an autobiography. People could choose whether to buy it. The BBC, however, derive much of their income through the sale of television licences to the public. The government forces taxpayers to cough up without giving them any say whatsoever in what is broadcasted into their homes. Taxpayers have no choice but to line my pockets with legitimately earned fees for my detailing my criminal exploits. This disturbed the BBC's conscience so much that the project never progressed beyond the script and music soundtrack stage for the next eighteen months, by which time Michael Wearing had left the BBC.

I felt it insane to let what is potentially a blockbuster movie to sit on the BBC's floor but began to think that they would never make a film of *Mr Nice*. It was too politically incorrect. I led a life of crime without doing that long in prison. I am still making money writing and talking about my past criminal adventures, and I am having a wonderful time. They do not make films about such people. If I became a grass, they would certainly make a film. They would if I died through drug abuse or if an envious dope gangster shot me.

Through a mutual friend, I met Sean Penn, who had earlier expressed an interest in making a film of *Mr Nice*. I had a first-class lunch with him in London. Sean was full of praises for my book, saying that he had already discussed its film potential with Hunter S Thompson, Woody Harrelson, and Mick Jagger. Sean followed up the meeting with this letter to the BBC:

> I am a great fan of Howard Marks's book *Mr Nice* and would like to offer my services to you as your American champion for the film. Please accept this letter as commitment of my continued support of the entire project up to and including joining your team of producers. I am willing to take an active role and I can confirm that I will utilise my experience, contacts and knowledge in order to bring this film to the international audience that I feel it deserves.
>
> Yours sincerely
>
> Sean Penn

The BBC was unimpressed with Sean's overtures. They did not even reply.

I was then utterly convinced that if a *Mr Nice* film would ever be shown in a cinema, it would be after my death. Rhys Ifans might be too old to play me.

In 1997, I was offered the job of columnist for *Loaded*, the first, and for several years, the most successful lads' magazine. I did it for five years. On one occasion, *Loaded* asked me to join the Stereophonics tour and interview them. I'd got it completely wrong. Reading about the Stereophonics in the music press had given me the idea that they were three straight non-smoking, possibly teetotal, well-behaved Welsh valley kids earnestly dedicated to bringing certain aspects of Welsh culture to the English and other foreigners. The Stereophonics had got it wrong, too. Reading about me in the music press had given them the idea that I was a possibly teetotal, well-over-the-hill hippie who had progressed from weed to heroin because his lungs had packed up. They were gloomily anticipating a barrage of dribbly questions about pissing against walls and shagging groupies behind slag heaps of sheep shit.

The venue was the De Montfort Hall, Leicester, a city of cheese and curry. Along came Jones, five foot six inches of pure fuse wire.

"Hello, butt. I'm Kelly. Have you seen those two guys who were shorter than me? I need people like that around me all the time. It is bad enough having a girl's name, let alone being the same size as one. So what do you want to interview us about, butt?"

"I hadn't actually got that far in my thinking, Kelly, but I suppose I should ask you some questions right now. Someone told me you've never really been into dance music, like house or garage or big beat. Why not?"

"Howard, if our older brothers heard us playing that, they'd smack our heads against the wall. We had to listen to Led Zeppelin until our ears bled, which they did. We had no choice, like."

"Why are you called the Stereophonics?"

"After Stuart's grandmother's gramophone."

"What about you, Stuart? What stuff did you listen to on your granny's record player?"

"Same as I do now, really, like all the boys: AC/DC, Kiss, Rush, Deep Purple, Lynyrd Skynyrd, Guns N' Roses, Led Zeppelin, Credence Clearwater, the Kinks, Stevie Wonder, Rainbow, Bad Company. They're all great. We still wear their T-shirts."

Then along came Jones, at least six foot of him this time.

"All right, How? I'm Richard, the bass player."

His hardcore tattoos reminded me of US penitentiary inmates, his unchanging deep eyes reminded me of a Thai mystic with whom I once spent some time.

"What music got you going, Richard, when you were a kid?"

"That's easy: ska and punk. Same as my three older brothers."

Cwmaman, like much of the south Wales valleys, had outlawed virtually all music made after 1979. Lack of community funds meant no money to sponsor visiting bands. Over 50 per cent unemployment meant no bus fare to go to Cardiff and no money for state-of-the-art valley blasters. The jukebox in the corner of the lounge bar provided all entertainment. However, some pub jukeboxes are better than others, and none even get close to those mechanical muses that still smoulder in the watering holes of the Welsh valleys.

Fame had gone completely to their heads, but not in the usual way. But with the Stereophonics, fame simply made them bored with celebrities and irritated with celebrity liggers. They were entirely unimpressed by the trappings of fame and refused to take any kind of advantage it might offer. For example, they gave up seats presented to them in the holy of holies executive section at the Wales v South Africa rugby game in order to sit with the boys. To ensure they did not yield to superstar status, they toured in a huge bus along with their family and a bunch of mates from Cwmaman. Where they go, the boys go too, and the boys make certain they stay grounded.

The Stereophonics casually ambled on stage to a cacophony of nubile adulation. They rubbed their lager bottles three times, and popped out the rock geniuses they had been given at birth. They were the next step up the evolutionary ladder of jukeboxes, a soulful, human and technically perfect example of what used to sit in the corner of the pub, blasting blue heartland rock. Richard pumped bass religiously while casually chatting to Stuart, who drummed faster than I could think. Ex-boxer, footballer, martial artist, scriptwriter, and current singer, songwriter, lead guitarist Kelly growled like an earthquake, a mad passionate sobbing roar with more overtones than a valley full of orchestras, male voice choirs, and rugby crowds.

Their success had exploded just two years previously in 1997 with the appropriately entitled *Word gets Around*, which yielded four top forty singles and gained immediate recognition as a musical and lyrical masterpiece. A couple more albums and they had become the rock band that shook and overcame the world.

The Stereophonics sincerely believe pub

regulars to be the best people in the world. They are the working-class heroes the Beatles (who played to the middle class) and the Rolling Stones (who were middle class) could never be.

Since then, the Stereophonics and I have attended each other's shows several times and we have shared wonderful nights of pure debauchery. They wrote and released a song about me – 'An Audience with Mr Nice', which was released as the B-side of 'Mr Writer', one of their biggest hits.

Stuart and Kelly fell out (but the friendship quickly resumed), and Stuart parted company from the other Stereophonics. Everyone who knew them was careful not to take sides. I continued to see each of them, taking great care to steer clear of the taboo subject of the other. Unannounced, Stuart once dropped round to see me in Kenfig Hill.

"Come on, 'Ow, answer the door, will 'ew?"

The voice was loud. Overtones of differing valleys' accents resonated deafeningly, vitalising the sleepy tranquillity of the street where I was born. The curtains of the houses across the road parted in concert. The neighbours had seen it all before – gangsters, spies, cops, Rastafarians, and men from Afghanistan, but they had never heard anything like this – Richard Burton in one ear, Tom Jones in the other, stereophonically balanced by wild Welsh wit.

"All right, 'Ow? 'Ow's it going? I thought you would never bloody answer. Shall we have a pint? Let's go to that pub you were on about, that one with a wall that talks in medieval Welsh."

We went to the Prince of Wales in Kenfig, Wales's most haunted pub. The regulars had seen it all. I had brought all sorts of celebrities, from famous film actors to sexy models, to this local pub. None had attracted more than passing glances. They were used to ghosts, for God's sake! However, when Stuart walked in, everyone immediately perceived he was one of their own. Within minutes, he was deep in animated jovial discussion with all of them.

When Stuart Cable left the Stereophonics, he embarked upon an extraordinarily successful career in TV and radio. His compassionate, humorous, humble, and well-grounded charisma invariably swamped audiences and guests, and his vibrant, impossible to dislike personality and unique voice made him an obvious front man for numerous charitable causes, work that he tenaciously continued right up to the end.

Stuart was the perfect master, exponent, and representative of Wenglish, a deliberately ignored dialect with its own unique vocabulary and consistent grammar spoken and understood by well over a million people living in the Welsh valleys. Wenglish began as the lingua franca of the mining valleys when they became the favoured destination of economic migrants from countries scattered throughout the world, and persists as a fusion of Welsh intonation with Welsh and immigrant English vocabulary. It is the grafters' Esperanto, the most diplomatic of all tongues. Until Stuart's work for *Cable TV* and *Kerrang!*, Wenglish had not streamed through the airwaves. If I had ever been asked to choose an ambassador for Wales, he would definitely have been on the short-list. I, and so many others, miss that hot-blooded hound of happiness.

# 11

# COOL CYMRU, PREJUDICES, AND MAM

I F I WASN'T in prison or in some remote part of the world, I would speak to my mother every day, taking my daily dose of Welsh, the only language we spoke with each other, the umbilical cord that tied me to the roots of my forefathers and to my childhood. After she died, I felt I had lost my direction as well as all my connections. I was on my own. Up until that point I had deliberately ignored all requests to do any media interviews in Welsh because there was too much Wenglish in my Welsh and my lack of vocabulary was the cause of great embarrassment to me.

But I changed my attitude. I didn't care anymore. It made no difference to me if I made some grammatical error or other or if I got the Welsh peculiarity, the mutations, wrong. I worried even less if I used English words in my Welsh conversation. My mother never bothered translating so many English words, such as submarine or nuclear physics. But there was nobody more Welsh than she was.

I took advantage of every opportunity to spend as much time as possible with people who were almost entirely Welsh speaking, like the Super Furries and Rhys Ifans. Speaking the language, even just hearing it, was enough to keep the spirit of my mother by my side. Sometimes, I would visit the market in Swansea, as she used to do. It was a delight to see the heart-shaped cockles and the laver bread glistening as black as the crow by its side. I would enjoy getting lost in the incessant chatter of the women who had just come back from scouring the sand and mud banks of the estuary at Penclawdd on the Gower Peninsula.

At the same time, I was finding it difficult putting this strong Welsh urge side by side with the Wales I had been desperate to leave when I was a teenager. There was no doubt that I was reconnecting myself to a definite Welshness. I wanted to keep my mother's Welsh spirit alive, in every sense of the word, but I didn't want to reconnect to her Wales.

When I lived in her home, I believed the best thing to come out of Wales was the M4, transporting me well away from that narrow, irrelevant and silly Wales. The inhabitants were puritanical, sadly lacking in self worth, and obsessed with mind-rotting triviality. The country was hopeless, irrelevant, and nowhere near cool.

During the premiere of *Mr Nice* in Cardiff, I did get a few glances of the former Wales, in particular the old Welsh puritanical attitude. Surprisingly, it came from one or two of the press who interviewed me in the Hilton Hotel during the afternoon before the premiere. There were overtones of an almost Nazi type attitude behind some questions about the 'message' the film gives and so on. But that would have been the general consensus in the past; today it's an exception and one which might have more to do with class than nationality.

But now, the country is alive. One giant cauldron of musical talent, mysticism and enthusiasm. Most certainly 100 per cent cool with no shortage of talent attracting the attention of the outside world. The rock stars, the beautiful women, the sporting champions from boxing to darts. And the nation has just hosted one of the biggest sporting events in the world, the Ryder Cup, which was a huge success, despite all talk of the weather. I don't think Wales has ever looked so good as it did in the eyes of the millions who saw this small country put on such a big show. As Colin Montgomerie, the captain of the European team said, "The whole word was watching and Wales delivered." It did for me too. What's happened then? Had Wales changed? Or was it me?

In many ways, Wales had clearly changed. The pits were gone and the chapels are disappearing just as fast. More people are speaking Welsh and devolution has happened. Wales had evolved to be a loosely independent country. Maybe the Cynulliad, the Assembly, deserves some praise for transforming the country despite the narrow majority in favour of setting it up.

On the other hand, one strong characteristic of independence is not to be in the position of feeling the need for it. A paradox for which there are three possible reasons. First, we Welsh are incredibly, spinelessly, servile – I don't think the Romans would agree. Second, we're completely unaware of what's going on, which is unlikely. Third, we are so confident that we shall overcome and so proud of our significance as a nation, we don't feel the need to kick-up a fuss purely because things have been difficult for a while.

No doubt the bad days will come again. But we are aware of that and we know ourselves. A few centuries of English force-feeding isn't going to change anything as going through slavery and imprisonment is an integral part of growing up.

There might not be any Welsh in the Houses of Windsor and Hanover, but 500 years ago the Tudors ruled the vast majority of the world. Since the days of the poet Taliesin and Merlin, we have known the red dragon will always slay the white one. Our day will come time and time again. My country has not dramatically changed. But my way of looking at it certainly has.

The change happened when I was in prison. A black gangster from Chicago, in jail for murdering a policeman, told me more about Wales than I had ever known before.

My knowledge up until then had been gained from living as a Welsh man in Wales for decades. His information was gleaned after a few accidental minutes listening to a radio programme in Indiana, the birth place of the Ku Klux Klan. It's another question why the radio station made a programme about Wales in the first place. I'll never know. But I must thank Tee Bone, the Lucifer who ignited my Welsh fires.

Discovering the influence the Welsh have had on the world, especially North and South America made me feel immensely proud. The libraries of the prison were able to help my process of discovery. Gradually, but indelibly, this triumphantly replaced the embarrassment I had felt about being Welsh.

I also feel all the researching, reading, and searching started at a period of my life when I had started to go on inward, spiritual journeys through my yoga and meditation. I was beginning not to take myself so seriously. I was starting to think more about other people. My roots, which were all over the place, were beginning to be grounded.

This new-found pride grew and strengthened as soon as I left prison. The research continued and took me to foreign lands; to Jamaica looking for connections with one of my great heroes, Henry Morgan the Welsh buccaneer, once the country's governor; to the Chubut Valley in Patagonia, Argentina, finding Welsh-speaking South Americans, where doors, closed for generations, opened to me.

Some of the main players on my journey of discovery have been friends for over a decade by now. Every one of them overflows with talent, life and fun. But they also have a strong, firm, continuing love for their country and their people. With enthusiasm and tenacity, they have succeeded in transmitting this joy and pride to the rest of the world. And on every step of the journey, everyone, everywhere has known clearly enough that each one of them was Welsh. I am so lucky to be able to share their optimism, their confidence, pride and spirit of fun.

Today, I am still captive to the most infectious Welsh enthusiasm, which shows itself in so many ways. Two years ago, my publishers commissioned me to write a series of crime fiction books. I decided immediately to locate and write those stories in Wales. I would never have considered doing so some years ago. The main character is a woman police officer in Cardiff and most of the action and excitement happens at Dinas Head and Cardiff.

Less than a year ago I had the wonderful opportunity of spending quite a bit of time in the valleys, on the film set of *Mr Nice*. It was a time with the people of the valleys and a time watching a good friend playing me in a film. Both contributed much to this process of further realising what Wales is today. Some months ago, Rhys and I sat nervously side by side to see the final version of the film, tentatively holding hands in the front row of the cinema where the showing was held. That backstage meeting at a Super Furries gig and the signing of the Rizla's had come full circle as indeed had my own journey to the roots of Wales and to my Welsh roots.

Finally, earlier on this year I had the opportunity of putting a book together in the Welsh language. I now have a book in Welsh with my name on the cover. It would have been a source of even greater pride and pleasure for my mother.

# AN OLD PUB, A PIRATE, AND JAMAICA

W HEN FILMING *MR Nice*, my oldest friend, Marty Langford, called me.

"Howard – just wanted to draw your attention to Llanrumney Hall."

"What's happening there, Marty?"

"It might have to close down. It's in a bad way, and the roof is leaking. They don't think they can get enough money to fix it."

"That's a massive shame, it can't close, surely? Isn't there some organisation that can step in?"

"The locals have already raised some money but there's loads more needed, and they can't do it. Simple as that. The brewery won't commit themselves either way at the moment."

No doubt there are several pubs in a similar situation in Wales, but Marty knew this particular one meant something special to me.

The pub in question boasts the grand name

Llanrumney Hall. Today it's in the Llanrumney suburb of Cardiff, but during the seventeenth century it lay in a small village between Newport and Cardiff. These days the pub is used by a handful of loyal locals needing a place to chew the fat and slake their thirst, a pensioners' group who meet for tea, and it serves as the headquarters of the village rugby club. The pub is a Grade I listed building, constructed in 1450 as the home of Squire Morgan, whose family crest still crowns one of the fire places. One of his descendants is my greatest Welsh hero – Captain Sir Henry Morgan, the seventeenth-century buccaneer who fought against the Spanish for control of the Caribbean and won. He was born in Llanrumney Hall and lived his early infant life there.

Sometime after the phone call I received an e-mail with a picture of the pub. It was in a sorry and neglected state, indicative of the peculiar attitude a lot of Welsh people show towards Henry Morgan. He is either romanticised as the pirate who became acting governor of Jamaica or ignored because his pirating exploits brought shame and dishonour in their wake, offending both puritanical and class sensibilities. It was the same attitude I came across when I visited a mansion house on the outskirts of Newport, Tredegar House. For over five hundred years this was the ancestral home of the Morgan family and is still open for guided tours. I had visited there with Marty a while ago. The portraits of each Morgan family member hanging in the grand rooms were proudly explained, but one was deliberately ignored.

"Who is this, then?" Marty just couldn't let things pass and, annoyingly for the guide, knew his stuff as well.

"Oh! That's Henry Morgan, a pirate and the black sheep of the family, we don't mention him."

"Looks a bit like you, Howard." Marty quipped before starting again on the guide.

"He was a bit more than a pirate, wasn't he? He was the governor of Jamaica."

"Deputy governor only, I think," she cut across him briskly.

"But he was knighted, wasn't he?"

"They did things like that in those days. All sorts could be knighted then."

She carried on showing us round the mansion, which in its day had welcomed colourful characters such as Alistair Crowley, H G Wells, Aldous Huxley, and George Bernard Shaw. More recently, the place has attracted the likes of the Hairy Bikers and Dr Who – the 2008 Christmas special was filmed there. But my interest remained in Henry Morgan, and the tour guide was helpful enough to inform us that Henry was born in Llanrumney Hall on the outskirts of Cardiff. She left us with one parting shot.

"You'll have no trouble believing he was born there: it's one of the roughest places in Wales."

Marty and I found the place sandwiched between a rugby pitch and a crack house estate. Helpful truanting children had directed us, but they had added one caution. The place was haunted by the ghost of a criminal who had been cut into pieces and buried in the cellar there. The criminal's name was Henry Morgan. It was good to know these 12-year-old boys knew his name, even if they were perpetuating one of many Henry Morgan myths.

There had been signs then that all was not right.

"What have you got to eat?" Marty asked the barman.

"Plain or cheese and onion," was the matter-of-fact reply.

But the Henry Morgan bug had bitten. I wanted to know more and began researching into his life and times. Writing this book gave me an excuse to go up again into the attic in Kenfig Hill and blow the dust off the boxful of notes on Henry Morgan.

Henry was the son of a scullery maid and a

143

gentleman farmer squire and was born in 1635 at Llanrumney Hall. As an infant, he was taken a little further north to Princeton, a small village lying between Merthyr Tydfil and Tredegar, then moved to the family's estate in Pencarn. An energetic and ambitious man, Henry embraced pleasure and detested any claims to the moral high ground, especially those made by the bigoted Puritans or the Roman Catholic Church. Seeking adventure, fame and fortune, he went to Bristol and gambled and brawled his way into and out of trouble.

A little later, another Welshman also left his home town to follow the same impulse. Beau Nash left Swansea to go to Bath and ended up as master of ceremonies in that Roman town. He was the master party organiser of his and succeeding generations. He controlled who was in Bath high society, but did much to make social events more accessible to the middle classes as well. He remembered his roots. He matched ladies with their dancing partners at the balls he organised, accompanied unescorted ladies, and brokered marriages. He was a notorious gambler, and the debts he incurred forced him to move in with his mistress, who was so distraught when he died she decided to live in a tree.

Henry Morgan, however, quickly left Bristol and joined the throngs making their way to meet the great demand for British labour in the plantations of the colonies. Much of this demand was satisfied by indentured servants, most of whom were offenders sentenced to penal servitude overseas, but some were tricked into indentured service by the promise of retirement in a tropical paradise. Whether as an indentured servant or the victim of a press-gang, records show that on 3 May 1655 Henry boarded a ship bound for the West Indies.

Typically, another unexpected phone call played its part in the next step of my discovering more about Henry's life and times. It was from Jeanette Hyde from the *Observer*. I'd written a few pieces for their travel section.

"We would like to send you on a trip again. This time, probably somewhere in South America – Brazil, Panama or Argentina. Take your pick."

This was the ideal opportunity to follow my obsession with Latin American connections and Welsh rogues. I could research my ancestry as well as recapture my childhood. I was not aware of any links between Wales and Brazil, so I put that country to the back of my mind. Panama or Argentina was the choice, and I went for Panama. I had met General Manuel Noriega in Miami Metropolitan Correctional Centre on my journey through the American justice system. He was the first leader of a country to declare war on the United States since the Second World War. The USA had killed thousands of Panamanian nationals, dumped them in mass graves and left tens of thousands impoverished and homeless. This had happened just a few months before I met Noriega. He started off on America's side, having first been trained by George Bush Snr when he was a CIA chief. But he switched sides, sold arms to Cuba, and trafficked drugs with the Colombian cartels. The USA's response was the first example of a now familiar policy of invading an entire country to capture one opponent. There was no chance I'd see Noriega in Panama: he was still in the federal penitentiary.

The flight itinerary for my Panamanian trip arrived. There was a problem.

"Jeanette, I can't do this trip. I have to change planes at Miami."

"And why is that a problem?"

"If I ever visit America, I'll be banged up forever."

I explained the parole situation: I was an aggravated felon. I could never set foot, inadvertently or otherwise, in the US. If I did, I'd never get out. Jeanette said she would re-work the schedule.

The new return ticket arrived in the post – I had to change in Jamaica. I was delighted. It was to be only an overnight stop each way, but that would be long enough to get a taste of rum, an earful of reggae, and a lungful of reefer. It was also Henry Morgan's favourite place on the planet.

I stayed in Jake's Hotel, Treasure Beach, a personal favourite of Robbie Williams and a member of the Island Resorts chain owned by Chris Blackwell, who founded Island Records in 1959. The rock 'n' roll hall of fame honours Blackwell as having done more than anyone else to bring reggae music to the world stage. His mum was of Jamaican ancestry, and she was credited by James Bond author, Ian Fleming, to have inspired the creation of his character Pussy Galore.

Blackwell was at one stage an aide-de-camp to the governor of Jamaica. Henry Morgan was the assistant governor (for a while the acting governor) of the same island, albeit a few hundred years earlier.

After setting up Island Records, Blackwell signed Welshman Spencer Davis, who had a string of hits with the Spencer Davis Group throughout the 1960s. Blackwell was also responsible for making Bob Marley the Third World's first superstar. One afternoon at the hotel library, I read about the man whom I had been aware of for decades and whose music I loved. In Jamaica's *Daily Post*, I was surprised to learn that he was of mixed race. His mother was a Jamaican, Ciddy Brooker, and she married Captain Norval Sinclair Marley, a British army officer who was the British West Indian regiment quartermaster. The marriage was a scandal, and the Marley family disinherited Norval. The story stated Norval Marley was born in Prestatyn, north Wales. I found it hard to believe what I was reading: Bob Marley was Welsh. I couldn't wait to tell the boys back home.

Leroy Bowen was a Jamaican with whom I had spent a lot of time in Terre Haute prison, mostly playing Scrabble, backgammon, and chess. We were deported on the same day from Oakdale Alien Detention Centre. His ancestors had gone the other way, from Jamaica to Wales. We have remained close friends ever since our release and now, on his home island, he was my guide.

We headed out of Kingston towards Port Royal.

"Wait until yo see dee name a dee hotel!"

I saw the name: Morgan's Harbour Hotel and Beach Club. At least there was acknowledgement of the great man's presence in the Caribbean, if not in Wales. A large picture of Henry Morgan dominated reception. Ripples of excitement tickled my stomach.

I was led to my room, which I was reliably informed was where a large spider attacked James

Bond in the film *Dr No*. I asked for plain lobster and any strong rum drink. The waiter brought over a frontend loader, compliments of the house. A frontend loader comprises overproof rum, pimento liquor, molasses, clear syrup and various roots with names such as cock-stiff, strong back, and genital root. Overproof rum is an integral part of Jamaica's pharmacopoeia and serves as an antiseptic. It also cures colds and fevers, and Henry Morgan used it as a virility aid. I downed another.

Henry Morgan, admiral of the Brethren of the Coast, was ceremoniously welcomed when he sailed into Port Royal with his treasure, but he had broken the 1670 Treaty of Madrid, in which England and Spain agreed to respect each other's territories in the Americas. This had been signed just before Henry sacked Panama, and Spain demanded the death penalty. Henry, suffering from a heavy fever, was arrested and put on board a leaky ship bound for London to face charges of treason. On arrival in England, he was immediately released on bail. At his trial there was no judge, no jury, no single witness. Henry proved he could not have known about the peace treaty with Spain, apologised for his ignorance, and left the court a free man.

In London, the freed Henry Morgan drank at the inns, smoked tobacco in the coffee houses, gambled at the races, attended the theatre, and journeyed to Wales for short vacations. Nobility welcomed him at their homes, where he entertained them with swashbuckling tales of adventure and romance. King Charles II and Henry became great friends. The king assisted Henry's wenching with court beauties, while Henry's street credibility enabled the king to engage in clandestine orgies at dockside taverns, grog shops, and brothels. Henry introduced the king to His Majesty's best-known mistress, the Welsh actress Nell Gwyn. Henry's health improved, and he begged the king to let him return to Jamaica, the island he loved. Charles II responded by knighting Henry and appointing him lieutenant-governor of Jamaica.

On his return to Port Royal, Henry formed his own political party, and became judge-admiral of the customs, dishing out fines and confiscating selected spoils. He was the official first citizen of Port Royal and was acting governor – effectively dictator – of Jamaica for two years.

Port Royal was now the richest city in the world, and dedicated to the disposal of plunder and providing a good time. Wearing London's fashion as they strolled down paved walkways, residents lived in luxuriously furnished cut-stone homes with fully stocked wine cellars, tiled roofs and sash windows. A synagogue, Quaker meeting house, Roman Catholic chapel, Presbyterian and Anglican churches evidenced Port Royal's religious toleration.

It was also the most wicked city in the world, whatever criterion one used. There were more taverns per head, more brothels per square yard, and more stolen goods than anywhere else before or since. Along the dockside, narrow alleys were lined with dirty houses offering every brand of vice ever invented. Fornicating took place on an unprecedented scale, encouraged by the House of Correction for Lazy Strumpets situated at the water's edge.

Highly sexed, Henry had his own harem and saw nothing immoral in taking full advantage of attractive young women of all races, preferably virgins. As for buccaneering, although he made secret deals with pirates and occasionally got them out of trouble, Henry didn't join their escapades. His offices ruled out undertaking any piracy, privateering, or aggression against Spain. Deprived of Henry's prior leadership, the Brethren of the Coast, the most powerful international criminal organisation ever, were giving way to a new breed of pirate – rogues, cut-throats, and other seafaring trash. Henry had no time for them. They had shown him their true colours: they were scum who couldn't take losses or show gratitude for sharing in someone else's good fortune. Henry was now getting into real crime, running a colony with the help of his mate the king of England. He took it easy and lay in his hammock on one of his plantations, drinking rum and inventing more cocktails.

Henry stamped out the use of Jamaica as a base for pirates and buccaneers, closing Port Royal to illegal craft, whether foreign or English, and imposed stringent checks on ships flying the flags of potential enemies of England. He issued an ultimatum to captains: seek pardon for their previous misdemeanours, promise never to indulge in such practices again, and buy cheap land in Jamaica – as he had done. Believing Henry Morgan would take such a course only if there was money to be made by it, the pirates became plantation owners – Jamaica's landed gentry.

Roman Catholic James II succeeded Protestant Charles II. Despite his affection for Spain, he was an avid fan of Henry and continued to support him. A Dutch attempt to discredit Henry by exposing him as a former criminal ended with Henry Morgan becoming the first person ever to be awarded monetary damages in a libel case.

Henry had now reached the peak of his power, but the challenges had run out. The thrill had gone. He developed swollen legs, a huge paunch, puffy eyes, and yellow skin. He lost his appetite. Age brought nothing with it but a restless waiting, a wish for peace and a dull expectancy of a state that could not be imagined. On 25 August 1685, Henry Morgan died of alcoholic poisoning and tuberculosis.

Leroy took me to see some of his friends, and with a spliff from one of them in my hand, we set out to look for traces of Henry Morgan's life on the island. I needed to find his main home on the island. We headed towards Jamaica's north-east coast. A few miles from the shore, Leroy stopped the car on a deserted main road.

"Llanrumney, mon."

I looked around. The countryside was green and beautiful, and the gentle hills and meadows reminded me of certain parts of Wales, but not the Cardiff suburb whose name it shared. There was nothing else to be seen.

"Are you sure, Leroy?"

"Me 100 per cent sure, mon. Believe me."

On the back of a tractor driven by Marvin, who lived nearby, we went further inland. After several attempts, we eventually crossed a river and motored slowly up a slight grassy incline. Near the top, the hill got steeper, so we abandoned the tractor and walked to the summit. It was covered with stone walls reduced to ruins a few feet high with some old cannon and other rusty bits and pieces. There were several small caves with boarded-up entrances. Marvin motioned me to follow him. Large red letters stood out from one of the walls. C-A-R-T-R-E-F spelt the Welsh word for home. I felt weird.

Marvin said the caves surrounding us went in labyrinthine fashion down to the sea, and there were still pieces of Morgan's treasure there for the taking, but it was too dangerous to get them.

I had expected to be thrilled by the experience of following in the footsteps of Henry Morgan, visiting the land he had chosen to remind him of his Welsh birthplace, let alone possibly discovering his treasure. Perhaps my unease arose from knowing Henry had lived there during his dotage, his period of disillusionment and paranoia, when he was surrounded by the ghosts of vanished thrills. He should have spent his last years in Wales, where the blood of his ancestors had soaked the soil to keep it Welsh for always.

Maybe I should buy that pub where he was born.

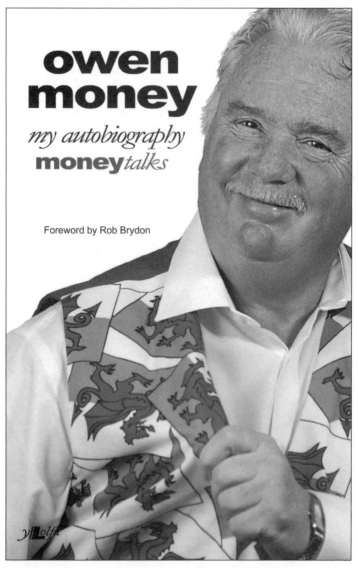

# Mal Pope

## Old Enough to Know Better

**My Autobiography**

y Lolfa

£9.95

Still Rockin'

TOM JONES
A BIOGRAPHY

y Lolfa

Aubrey Malone

£6.95

# OPERATION
# Julie

### Lyn Ebenezer

## The World's
## Greatest **LSD** Bust

### y Lolfa

£9.95

This book is just one of a whole range of
publications from Y Lolfa. For a full list of
books currently in print, send now for your
free copy of our new full-colour catalogue.
Or simply surf into our website

# www.ylolfa.com

for secure on-line ordering.

TALYBONT CEREDIGION CYMRU SY24 5HE
*e-mail* ylolfa@ylolfa.com
*website* www.ylolfa.com
*phone* (01970) 832 304
*fax* 832 782